D0287542

THIS DAY IN
PHILADELPHIA
SPORTS

BY BRIAN STARTARE AND KEVIN REAVY

Foreword by Charlie Manuel

SPORTS
PUBLISHING

Kevin—

To my extraordinary mother, my biggest fan. And my father, who has forgotten more about sports than I'll ever know.

Brian—

To my boys Chase and Braydon, for my love of Philadelphia sports is only surpassed by the immense love I have for you both.

Copyright © 2014, 2016 by Brian Startare and Kevin Reavy

All Rights Reserved. No part of this book may be reproduced in any manner without the express written consent of the publisher, except in the case of brief excerpts in critical reviews or articles. All inquiries should be addressed to Sports Publishing, 307 West 36th Street, 11th Floor, New York, NY 10018.

Sports Publishing books may be purchased in bulk at special discounts for sales promotion, corporate gifts, fund-raising, or educational purposes. Special editions can also be created to specifications. For details, contact the Special Sales Department, Sports Publishing, 307 West 36th Street, 11th Floor, New York, NY 10018 or sportspubbooks@skyhorsepublishing.com.

Sports Publishing® is a registered trademark of Skyhorse Publishing, Inc.®, a Delaware corporation.

Visit our website at www.sportspubbooks.com.

10 9 8 7 6 5 4 3 2 1

Library of Congress Cataloging-in-Publication Data is available on file.

Color Commentary headshots: Kevin Reavy: Michael Kirk, Bradcam Imaging
Brian Startare: Courtesy of Brian Startare

Cover design by Owen Corrigan
Cover photo credit: top Michael Kirk and bottom © AP Images

ISBN: 978-1-61321-841-9
Ebook ISBN: 978-1-61321-842-6

Printed in the United States of America

ACKNOWLEDGMENTS

Sports history, like all history, is definite to a degree, but ever-evolving.

The constant changes, updates, adjustments, and new discoveries made for quite an undertaking for this project, and it wouldn't have been possible without the help of so many great people:

Mike Kirk, for his assistance in editing, fact checking, and photography.

Ted Silary, for his vast Philly high school expertise, and generosity.

Tim Wiles of the National Baseball Hall of Fame and Museum, for going above and beyond in finding information in hard to reach places.

Julie Ganz, for her tireless work and reliable assistance.

Charlie Manuel for a tremendous, heartfelt foreword.

Ray Didinger, for his Hall of Fame advice and setting the example for excellence in sports journalism.

And a huge thank you to the following for their support, advice, guidance, and assistance in the creation of this project:

Missy Martin, David Christ, Dr. Richard Lamberski, Dr. Mary Beth Leidman, Bobby Shantz, Robert Melso,

Cindy Webster, The Philadelphia Eagles, The Philadelphia Flyers, Glen Macnow, Brian Propp, Jay Halligan, Derek Rodenbeck, and a host of others along the way. If we missed your name, blame our editor, but know we appreciate all of you.

A note from Brian:

I would like to thank my family for their support and understanding. It is quite difficult to juggle multiple jobs and projects without having a patient support system. Thank you specifically to my wife Andrea, and my sons Chase and Braydon. Thank you to all of my family members and friends for their support and encouragement, as I continue on with this most demanding but rewarding career.

A note from Kevin:

I would like to thank my friends and family for their support and patience in waiting out a seemingly endless project. Specifically, my stepfather, Dave, for making this possible, and my stepmother, Linda, for her encouragement along the way. Her spirit and memory was an inspiration, as it remains now and forever.

TABLE OF CONTENTS

FOREWORD

"**T**his is for Philadelphia!"

It felt so good to utter those words up on that stage the night we won the World Series. And you know what? I meant every word.

I came to Philadelphia in 2003 as an advisor with the Phillies, and was excited to be in the City of Brotherly Love. During that time, working in the organization and closely with the minor leagues, I knew we were on the cusp of doing big things. I witnessed our core coming up, growing together, and when I became the manager of the club in 2005, I just knew Philadelphia was where it was going to happen. I just had that feeling.

I've heard plenty about the reputation of Philadelphia, that it was a tough, blue-collar town, and that the fans could be rough. Well, let me tell you, the fans were rough, tougher than I ever imagined. However, they created the energy, the atmosphere, and were the driving force behind our ascent. I cherished every moment, even the most difficult ones. The hard times make you stronger.

After the great finish of the 2007 regular season when we caught the Mets, we lost three straight to Colorado. But after that series, my expectations for this club got real, real big, as did the fans'. However, I knew if my team played hard and put a good product out on the field, with maximum effort and hustle, the fans would respond. And did they ever.

I've been to other baseball cities. Everyone in baseball knows the east is tough. Boston, New York, Cleveland, but it's the winning that counts. I was told by many that if I won in Philadelphia, I would see a party that I would never, ever forget. And boy were they ever right.

When I was asked to recall my fondest memory from my time in the city, it was an easy answer. The moment Brad Lidge struck out Eric Hinske of Tampa Bay, the building shook. As the players celebrated on the field, and the fans went crazy in the stands, I sat there in the dugout and watched. I wanted to take it all in. Then October 31st, 2008, was about as good as it gets. All those people wearing red, leaning down to shake their hands, they were just so appreciative. I was so very happy for them and the city.

Philadelphia is a fantastic town. It truly is a brotherhood. The fans are fueled by their sports teams. Even before I got there, I was a fan of Moses Malone, Billy Cunningham, and the 76ers. I always marveled at how the bars were always packed for Flyers games. The Eagles and their great run. I pulled for Andy Reid, as he did for me. I enjoyed it all—the fans, the city, its history—and loved being a part of it.

And that's why you'll enjoy this book. Three hundred sixty-five days of Philadelphia historical sporting events. I hope it brings back memories, the good and the bad. It was very tough saying goodbye to the city [as manager], but I hope the fans will remember me as a winner, remember the fun times, when the Phillies won the city over. I'll remember you as well. I consider myself fortunate to have won in Philadelphia, to be part of a winning legacy, together with the fans, forever, and I'm glad I'm able to remain a part of this organization.

Enjoy Philadelphia!
—Charlie Manuel, January 2014

1st

1935—Once upon a time, the Temple University Owls football program was a regional powerhouse in college football.

On this New Year's Day in 1935, the undefeated Owls (7-0-2), headed by Hall of Fame coach Glenn "Pop" Warner, played in the inaugural Sugar Bowl game, resulting in a 20-14 loss to Tulane (9-1).

2nd

2005—After suffering a 38-10 loss to the Cincinnati Bengals, the Philadelphia Eagles, who had rested their starters, finished the season with the top playoff seed, a first-round bye, and a 13-3 overall record—the Birds' best mark since the 16-game schedule was instituted in 1978. Donovan McNabb, enjoying his most successful season in Eagles green, became the first NFL quarterback to complete a season with more than 30 touchdown passes and less than 10 interceptions (31 TD/8 INT).

2015—In a dramatic front office shake-up, Eagles owner Jeffrey Lurie decided to grant complete control over all football-related decisions to Chip Kelly, essentially giving Kelly the dual role of head coach and general manager. This decision came at the expense of Lurie's handpicked right-hand man, Howie Roseman, who was stripped of his general manager duties and promoted to Executive Vice President of Football Operations.

3rd

1981—By way of a 31-16 win over the Minnesota Vikings, the Eagles won their first Divisional round playoff game (and second playoff victory overall) in franchise history.

The team was headed to its first Conference Championship and, ultimately, first Super Bowl, under the tutelage of fifth-year coach Dick Vermeil.

4th

1997—The Flyers rallied from a three-goal deficit, with two goals late in the third period, to tie the Colorado Avalanche at four in Denver. Trent Klatt and Mikael Renberg scored just 2:11 apart as the Flyers extended their unbeaten streak to 16 games, ending a six-game road trip.

The Flyers would upend the Boston Bruins a few nights later to stretch the mark to 17 (14-0-3), but the streak ended on home ice January 9th in a 3-1 defeat at the hands of the Tampa Bay Lightning.

5th

1991—In the long, storied history of the Philadelphia Eagles, "NFC Championship game" evokes stomach-churning emotions, a reflection of continuously (and consecutively) coming up short on the big stage. Well, before the Eagles' three straight NFC Championship game losses, there were three straight *Wild Card* game losses.

On this date in history, Buddy Ryan coached his last game with the Eagles, losing to the Washington Redskins 20-6 in the Wild Card round, to complete the hard-luck trilogy.

2009—After 11 years with Philadelphia (the Phillies made him the top pick of the 1998 MLB draft), Pat Burrell signed a free agent contract with the team he helped beat in the 2008 World Series, the Tampa Bay Rays.

Burrell's 251 home runs in a Phillies uniform are good for fourth-most in team history (Mike Schmidt, 548; Ryan Howard, 311 through 2013; Del Ennis, 259). But there were as many valleys in Burrell's Philly career as there were peaks.

Batting .221 in '09, Burrell hit just 14 home runs for his new team.

6th

1962—The Eagles played for the honor of third place.

From 1960 to 1970, the second-place finishers of each conference played a third-place game, The Pro Playoff Classic (also known as the Bert Bell Benefit Bowl, in honor of the Eagles' founding owner).

A year after winning the NFL Championship, the Eagles were blown out by the Lions, 38-10, giving Detroit the league's charitable consolation.

7th

1996—For the second time in three years, the Dallas Cowboys knocked the Eagles out of the playoffs. Dallas beat up on the Birds, 30-11, in the Divisional Round—a momentum-carrying win that would lead the way to Dallas' fifth Super Bowl victory.

Forced into the game after an early injury to starting quarterback Rodney Peete, then-backup QB Randall Cunningham struggled, completing just 42% of his passes in his last game as an Eagle.

8th

1995—His first time on the ballot, receiving 96.5% of the vote (third highest at the time), Phillies great Mike Schmidt was elected to the National Baseball Hall of Fame.

The 12-time All-Star, 10-time Gold Glove winner, and three-time National League MVP, Schmidt is the Phillies' career home run (548) and RBI (1,595) leader. But that's not all...

Schmidt is also the franchise leader in games played, at-bats, plate appearances, runs scored, hits, walks, total bases, runs created, sacrifice flies, and most times mentioned as the Phillies' all-time greatest player.

All this from a player not selected until the second round of the 1971 MLB draft—the Phillies' first round selection, RHP Roy Thomas, never played a game for Philadelphia.

9th

1991—Michael Jordan of the Chicago Bulls scored 40 points in a 107-99 win over the 76ers at the Spectrum, reaching the 15,000-point mark in his 460th game. Jordan was the second fastest to reach the mark in NBA history, next to Wilt Chamberlain (358 games).

Not to be confused with the youngest—Lebron James of the Cleveland Cavaliers holds the record, scoring his 15,000th NBA point in 540 games, before his 26th birthday.

10th

1918—The Philadelphia Athletics ball club was a volatile franchise. When it was good, it was great, winning five World Series before the Phillies could claim just its second *league* pennant. When it was bad, it was putrid.

The $100,000 Infield, with outfielder Eddie Murphy. From left to right: Stuffy McInnis, Murphy, Frank Baker, Jack Barry, Eddie Collins. *(Library of Congress)*

Known for making bold moves for short spurts in championship runs, the Athletics were similarly famous for suddenly drastically cutting costs for indefinite periods of rebuilding.

The latter was the case on this date in 1918, as the A's traded Stuffy McInnis (to the Boston Red Sox for Larry Gardner, Tilly Walker, and Hick Cady), the last holdover from owner Connie Mack's *$100,000 Infield*. The vaunted quartet, the core of the A's three championship teams in four years (1910–11, 1913), consisted of McInnis, Eddie Collins, Jack Barry, and Frank "Home Run" Baker.

Not surprisingly, the group's *100k* nickname became more of a hindrance for Mack, as he ultimately saw the group as more of a financial obstacle than a field spectacle.

11th

1960—Richie Ashburn's time in Philadelphia began in 1948, his All-Star rookie season, and ended in the broadcast booth in 1997.

But Ashburn wasn't always a Phillie. On this date in 1960, the Phils traded Whitey to the Chicago Cubs following a disappointing 1959 campaign. The following three-year span that ended his career was the only time Ashburn was not employed by the Phillies.

Following the 1962 season, Ashburn retired after hitting .306 for the Mets' inaugural season.

The following year, he joined Bill Campbell and Byrum Saam in the Phillies broadcast booth.

Richie Ashburn poses with Del Ennis and Bill Nicholson. *(Courtesy of the Boston Public Library, Leslie Jones Collection.)*

1976—There is a sense of pride that goes with Philly's greatest underdog, Rocky Balboa, defeating Ivan Drago of the Soviet Union during bitter Cold War times. But of course, that was all just movie make-believe (sorry, Rock, we still love you). And while *Rocky IV* is a TBS rerun powerhouse to whet our Soviet-squashing appetites, nothing beats the real thing.

The real thing in Philadelphia occurred on this day, as the Flyers handed the vaunted Soviet Red Army squad (CSKA) its first and only loss in the '76 Super Series four-game exhibition. Undefeated in stops at New York, Boston, and Montreal, the Soviet team was confident, but knew it was facing a new breed, squaring off against a Philly team they had called "animals," playing "rude hockey."

Ultimately, its pre-game prodding via the media turned to in-game protest on the ice, as the Soviets marched to the locker room midway through the first period after a crushing blow to star forward, Valeri Kharlamov, went unpenalized.

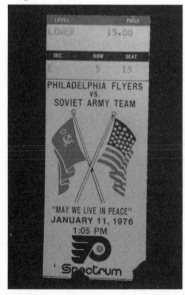

But after threats from team owner, Ed Snider, to withhold payment from the Soviet visitors, the Red Army meekly marched back onto the ice, eventually falling to Philadelphia, 4-1.

Broad Street Bullies 1, Communism 0.

2004—Down three points with 1:12 remaining and no timeouts, the Eagles were faced with 4th and 26 in the Divisional Playoff matchup

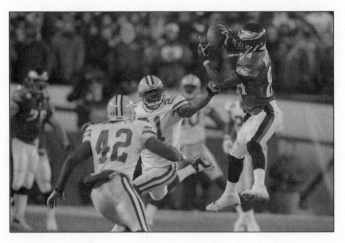

(Philadelphia Eagles)

with the Green Bay Packers. In one of maybe two relevant catches of his career, Freddie Mitchell caught the Donovan McNabb delivery just over the first-down marker to give the Birds new life.

The impossible conversion set up David Akers' 37-yard field goal, which tied the game at 17 and sent it into overtime.

COLOR COMMENTARY

Honestly, I thought the game was over, and so did everyone else. Another in a series of crushing postseason defeats. 4th and 26 with 1:12 left on the clock, and of course the Eagles with zero timeouts remaining. The Linc was emptying out. The fans were just disgusted. How could it end this way?

And then, the unthinkable happened. The Packers, for whatever reason, slipped back into their Cover 2 defense, leaving McNabb too much space to deliver the first down pass to Fred Ex. It was like a shot of adrenaline. We had hope again! A few plays later, David Akers drilled a game-tying FG, and then of course won the game in OT!

Out of the hundreds of Eagles games that I have attended over the years, this one had that serendipitous feel to it. It's meant to be! Of course, that feeling ended a week later in yet another NFC loss against Carolina. But hey, we beat Favre!

With that, a familiar playoff interception thrown by Brett Favre set up an Akers 31-yarder to ice it. Eagles 20, Packers 17.

12th

1994—Garnering 95.6% of the vote, Steve Carlton gained acceptance into the National Baseball Hall of Fame.

The Phillies' most prolific hurler, Lefty retired from baseball with 329 wins, 4,136 strikeouts (second only to Nolan Ryan at the time), and the most Cy Young awards (four) than any player in history (currently tied with Greg

Carlton, speaking at his Hall of Fame induction in Cooperstown, NY. *(Rubenstein)*

Maddux, and bested by Randy Johnson's five and Roger Clemens' seven).

Given the honor is voted on by the Baseball Writers Association of America, Carlton, who shunned the press the final ten years of his career, was a bit surprised by his landslide selection—

"It's like Rush Limbaugh being voted in by the Clintons."

13th

2007—With Donovan McNabb out for the season, backup quarterback Jeff Garcia started the final six games for the Eagles—a stretch in which the team went 5-1 with momentum carrying into the playoffs. But the up and coming New Orleans Saints ended the Birds' unlikely journey on this day in '07, besting Philly 27-24 in the divisional round.

Shibe (left, front row), playing host to fellow Major League executives, takes in the action from Game 2 of the 1913 World Series between the A's and New York Giants (*Bain News Service*)

14th

1922—Athletics president and part-owner Ben Shibe, 84, died on this date in 1922. The namesake of the Philadelphia As' and Phillies' Shibe Park, Shibe's contributions to the game extend well beyond city limits.

During his time with the A.J. Reach Sporting Goods Company (see January 24th) in Philadelphia, he invented the machinery to make the first standardized baseballs.

So, while Cooperstown might be the birthplace of baseball, Philadelphia (thanks in part to Shibe), it can be said, is the birthplace of *the* baseball.

15th

1965—In one of the most influential trades in basketball history, the San Francisco Warriors traded Wilt Chamberlain to the 76ers for Paul Neumann, Connie Dierking, Lee Shaffer, and $150,000. The move returned Chamberlain, the world's greatest basketball talent, to his roots of Philadelphia (where he had starred in high school and for the east-coast Warriors) and immediately legitimized the upstart Sixers franchise.

(Library of Congress)

Interestingly, both teams had the right idea. The Sixers immediately improved to 55-25 in '66 (from 40-40 the previous year), Chamberlain's first full season back in Philly. Similarly, the Warriors climbed to 35-45 in '66 (from a disastrous 17-63 in '65). But it was the '67 campaign which would literally determine the winner and loser of the trade.

The Sixers (68-13) and Warriors (44-37) met in the '67 Finals (see April 24th), with the Sixers winning the series 4-2, for the franchise's second championship and first in Philadelphia.

16th

2001—Wilt Chamberlain (he comes up a lot in this book) wasn't the only Philadelphia-area athlete to score 100 points in a game.

On this date in '01, Dajuan Wagner scored 100 points for Camden High in a 157-67 annihilation of Gloucester Township Tech. The local playground legend didn't need the achievement to build nationwide attention (some had already considered him the nation's top high school player), but it certainly didn't hurt.

After one collegiate season at Memphis, Wagner was selected by the Cleveland Cavaliers with the sixth overall pick in the 2002 NBA draft.

17th

2006—The United States unveiled their final preliminary roster for the first-ever World Baseball Classic.

Established as a response to baseball being removed from Olympic competition, the WBC has grown huge in popularity, specifically internationally. The '06 and '09 finals delivered some of the highest sporting event ratings in Japanese television history.

Brett Myers, Jimmy Rollins, and Chase Utley made the first roster on this date, but Utley was the only remaining Phillie to don the Team USA jersey in the WBC.

Internationally, the Phillies organization was well represented:

Rheal Cormier, Scott Mathieson (Canada); Carlos Ruiz (Panama); Pedro Feliz, Robinson Tejeda, Eude Brito (Dominican Republic); and Tomas Perez (Venezuela) all participated.

18th

2004—The Birds lost their *third straight* NFC Championship game, this time to the Carolina Panthers, 14-3.

With running back, and safety net, Brian Westbrook on the sideline nursing an injury, Donovan McNabb was intercepted four times (thrice by Panthers cornerback Ricky Manning, Jr.).

The signing of Terrell Owens was a forceful and effective reaction to a third-straight NFC Championship loss. *(Philadelphia Eagles)*

Clearly, Eagles receivers James Thrash and Freddie Mitchell were not getting the job done. This time, though, head coach Andy Reid got the message loud and clear.

In the offseason, Reid signed the volatile, but phenomenal, wide reciever Terrell Owens, and a trip to the Super Bowl was finally in the works.

19th

1981—On this date, the Oakland Raiders appeared on the cover of *Sports Illustrated*, under the heading, *"BRING ON THE EAGLES!"*

There would be no *SI* cover jinx here—The Raiders defeated the Birds (see January 25th) 27-10 in Super Bowl XV.

2003—As Brian Mitchell returned the opening kick deep into Tampa Bay Buccaneers territory, followed by a 20-yard touchdown run by Duce Staley, hopes were high that the Eagles would finally, rightfully, punch their ticket to Super Bowl XXXVII.

But that was the lone Eagles highlight in a frustrating 27-10 defeat to Tampa Bay—the second in a string of three straight NFC Championship losses for the club.

COLOR COMMENTARY

Out of all the postseason losses under Andy Reid, this one hurt the most, even more than the Super Bowl. In fact, it has been called

"Black Sunday" in Philadelphia, and is widely regarded as the worst loss in Philadelphia sports history.

It was all there for the taking. Tampa Bay had never won a game when the game time temperature was under 32 degrees, they never had a road playoff win, and the Eagles had their number, winning the last four contests between them. It was also the last football game ever at the Vet. It was a confluence of so many positive vibes. This was the Eagles' year.

And the game started off great for the Eagles—Brian Mitchell had a great kick return and then Duce Staley popped in a 20-yard touchdown, and the place was going bonkers. But that's where the story turns to despair. Bad memories include Joe Jurevicius running marathons on the Vet turf, many stalled Eagles drives in Bucs territory, and Ronde Barber going 92 yards on an interception return to cement another heartbreaker in Philly.

I still remember how silent the place was, and I still recall the final walk down The Vet's concourse ramps. In fact, it hurts just to write this.

An early lead, home field advantage, and a seemingly favorable matchup had been squandered, as 66,713 fans filed out of Veterans Stadium for the last time, having witnessed, arguably, the most devastating loss in franchise history.

20th

1983—No matter that Darryl Sittler garnered most of his NHL points donning the Toronto Maple Leafs' blue and white. On this date, during his first full season with the Flyers, Sittler scored his 1,000th NHL point.

Sittler's second-period goal in the Flyers' 5-2 victory over the Calgary Flames netted Sittler the career mark, making him just the second player in franchise history to score his 1,000th point with the team (Bobby Clarke the other), and the 17th player in NHL history to reach the milestone.

21st

1958—For one season, the Phillies held an exclusive National League TV deal in the Big Apple.

With the Brooklyn Dodgers and New York Giants bolting for the west coast, the Phillies agreed on this date to televise half their games in New York, which was suddenly devoid of an NL squad.

22nd

1992—Of all the career records established by the 76ers, one might think the career rebounding mark would belong to the 7'1" Wilt Chamberlain—a man who once pulled down an unfathomable 55 rebounds (see November 24th) in one game. But, in a 119-109 victory over the New York Knicks, Charles Barkley snagged his 6,642nd board, for the Sixers career mark, ahead of Hall of Famers Chamberlain and Billy Cunningham. Barkley finished the season, and his Philadelphia career, with 7,079 rebounds, which still stands as the team record.

23rd

2005—The Eagles had *finally* broken through, defeating the Atlanta Falcons, 27-10, in the painfully pesky NFC

Championship. The team's fourth straight trip to the conference title game was its first victory of the stretch, and second trip to the Super Bowl in team history (the other came in 1981).

The Birds, of course, lost Super Bowl XXXIX, but fielded a team widely considered among the greatest in the city's history.

Terrell Owens had 1,200 yards receiving and 14 touchdowns in his first season with Philly, and Donovan McNabb flourished with the extra help, having his best statistical season in pro football.

COLOR COMMENTARY

Another of those games where the apprehension was just so thrilling. It was the fourth straight season the Eagles were knocking on the door to the Super Bowl, but finally, this time, they kicked it in.

The whole afternoon had a different feel than the prior three occasions had.

Even without Terrell Owens, who was still recovering from injury, the entire line just felt confident. There were a lot of memories to take from that day, but the pure relief of finally getting over the hump was the one that will stick with me forever. The glitter, the confetti, the chill in the air, and nearly 68,000 in the stadium all shedding tears of joy. Finally!

Eagles owner, Jeffrey Lurie, with the George Halas Trophy, awarded to the NFC's best.
(Philadelphia Eagles)

24th

1900—The A. J. Reach Sporting Goods Company, based in Philadelphia and headed by Phillies founder A. J. Reach and A's owner Ben Shibe, received a patent (along with inventor Frank Mogridge) for the "Reach Pneumatic Head Protector." The rubbery blow-up head gear never caught on in Major League Baseball, but is credited as baseball's first protective batting helmet.

The A. J. Reach Company merged with Spalding in 1934.

25th

1981—The Eagles were 12-4 during the '80–'81 season, winning the NFC East and defeating the Cowboys, 20-7, in the Conference Championship to reach their first Super Bowl. The Oakland Raiders, however, spoiled the Dick Vermeil–coached team's shot at its first Lombardi Trophy on this day. With the 27-10 victory, the Raiders became the first NFL Wild Card team to win it all.

The loss for the Eagles abruptly ended a magical season.

COLOR COMMENTARY

The 1980–81 team has, mostly, been let off the hook by Andy Reid's "close enough" era of Eagles football, and perhaps rightfully so. There's something appealing about the lighting-in-a-bottle scenario, especially when the underdog falls just short of immortality (think the '93 Phils, or Rocky). It triggers our empathy more than our angst.

Over the years, '81 Super Bowl quarterback, Ron Jaworski, and head coach, Dick Vermeil, have been lauded as Philadelphia sports icons and local marketing studs (think Blue Cross/Blue Shield billboards and AAMCO commercials).

Somehow I doubt Donovan McNabb and Andy Reid will get the same kind of treatment.

26th

1931—Buzz Arlett, "The Babe Ruth of the Minor Leagues," was sold to the Philadelphia Phillies, after dominating for over a decade from the pitching mound and the batter's box, with the independent Oakland Oaks. Placed on waivers by Philadelphia at the end of his lone 1931 campaign, Arlett would never play in The Show again.

Hitting .313 in his only season in Major League Baseball, Arlett still holds the NL record for hits in a season by a one-year player (131).

Among minor leaguers, Arlett currently ranks third in home runs (432) and second in RBI (1,786). Terrible defensive play was Arlett's main obstacle toward garnering a long-term stay in the bigs.

Just a case of bad timing—the Designated Hitter, an idea originally conjured by the A's Connie Mack, wasn't instituted in the majors until 1973.

27th

1927—Major League Baseball commissioner, Kenesaw "Mountain" Landis, cleared Philadelphia A's outfielder Ty

Cobb, second in career hits in MLB history, was just as famous for his surly, bitter demeanor off the field (*Library of Congress*)

Cobb, and the Washington Senators' Tris Speaker, of fixing games.

The players' main accuser, Dutch Leonard, a longtime nemesis of the famously callous Cobb, failed to show up to the hearing, supposedly fearing a physical altercation with the ironically named "Georgia Peach."

28th

1901—The American League was formed, with the Philadelphia Athletics as one of the initial expansion franchises.

The league brought in former Pirates skipper Connie Mack to head the A's.

Mack, a notoriously shrewd businessman, raided the Phillies roster his first year as boss. When Pennsylvania contractual law sided with the Phils, Mack quickly swapped players to Cleveland (outside PA jurisdiction) for a return on his swindle.

Mack, "The Grand Old Man of Baseball." *(Paul Thompson)*

1958—In the 21st round of the NFL Draft, the Philadelphia Eagles selected John Madden (244th overall). Yes, *that* John Madden.

If you don't remember Madden ever playing for the Birds, that's because he never played a down of professional football. A knee injury ended his playing career in training camp, and his Hall of Fame coaching career was off the ground just a year later as an assistant at Allan Hancock College.

Madden coached the Oakland Raiders to victory over the Minnesota Vikings in Super Bowl XI.

Perhaps his greatest legacy, though? Headlining EA Sports' revolutionary football video game title, "Madden NFL Football."

29th

1993—610 AM/94.1 FM WIP's first Wing Bowl took place at the Wyndham Franklin Plaza in Philadelphia.

It started amidst a downturn in Eagles history, as sports radio hosts Al Morganti and Angelo Cataldi concluded that championship-challenged Philadelphia needed a bowl of its own.

They came up with what eventually became one of competitive eating's top events.

The first Wing Bowl took place in a hotel lobby, two contestants vying for the title of Philly's top glutton, and just 150 spectators in attendance. Carmen Cordero won the title, eating 100 wings, taking home a hibachi as his prize.

Today, over 20,000 fans pack the Wells Fargo Center in Philadelphia each year on the eve of Super Bowl weekend to witness 20+ contestants eat it out for a top prize, which usually includes a new set of wheels and thousands in cash.

30th

1948—Phillies general manager Herb Pennock, 53, died of a brain hemorrhage, igniting support for his Hall of Fame selection a month later.

Pennock, twice a 20-game winner, pitched 22 years in the majors, for the New York Yankees, Boston Red Sox, and Philadelphia Athletics.

A's left hander (1912–15) and Phillies general manager (1943–48) Herb Pennock (*Bain News Service*)

31st

2002—Harry the K and the Phillie Phanatic were Hall of Fame–bound.

On this date, Phillies broadcasting legend Harry Kalas was announced the winner of the Hall of Fame's Ford C. Frick Award, bestowed for lifetime achievement in broadcasting. In addition, the Phanatic, the Phils' lovable mystery mammal, would join the San Diego Chicken and the Expos' Youppi! as Major League Baseball's only mascots on display at the Hall's Museum.

1st

1973—In a late-January game against the Pittsburgh Penguins, Flyers defenseman Barry Ashbee, upset with being called for a penalty, struck the referee, knocking him to the ice.

What kind of penalty did the league implement for such actions back then? Clearly a sign of the times, Ashbee received just an eight-game suspension, and $150 in fines.

2nd

1968—Wilt Chamberlain's 100-point game is his most famous achievement (see March 2nd)—but is it his most impressive?

In a 131-121 win over the Detroit Pistons, Wilt collected 22 points, 25 rebounds, and 21 assists. It was the first and only double-triple-double in NBA history.

3rd

1976—In this *year*—chalk it up to the bicentennial—the NHL, NBA, and MLB All-Star games were held in Philadelphia.

On this *date*, the Spectrum hosted the NBA's East vs. West mid-season spectacle, with the East coming out on top, 123-109.

Dave Bing took MVP honors, playing alongside a slew of Hall of Famers, including Kareem Abdul-Jabbar, Rick Barry, Bob McAdoo, John Havlicek, Walt Frazier, Tiny Archibald, Elvin Hayes, and Dave Cowens.

4th

1991—The Hall of Fame voted to formally prohibit players on Major League Baseball's banned list from being considered for induction by the Baseball Writers Association of America (BBWAA) vote, the Hall's primary method for induction.

The Hall made the ruling as a reaction to the banning of Pete Rose, the only expelled player who would have met all other BBWAA ballot requirements.

Rose, the gritty leader of the Phils' 1980 championship team, was banned from baseball in 1989 by league commissioner Bart Giamatti for betting on baseball, or, as Giamatti put it, for having "engaged in a variety of acts which have stained the game."

5th

1880—The National League voted in the Worcester Ruby Legs (aka Worcesters/Brown Stockings). For two years, they'd serve as a placeholder team for the upcoming Philadelphia Quakers/Phillies.

Due to poor attendance in 1882, the Ruby Legs folded and Philly businessman Al Reach purchased the vacant spot for the would-be Phillies franchise. The Ruby Legs squad is historically distinct from the current Philly club, as only Worcester's reservation in the National League was for sale, not the team itself.

6th

1997—The Flyers' vaunted "Legion of Doom" line (see February 11) had its fair share of great games, but none better, statistically, than on this day.

From left to right: LeClair, Lindros, and Renberg. *(Philadelphia Flyers)*

The line, consisting of center Eric Lindros (one goal, four assists), and wingers John LeClair (four goals, two assists) and Mikael Renberg (one goal, four assists), set a team record for points by a single line (16). John LeClair set new single-game personal bests in both goals and points in the contest, a 9-5 win over the Montreal Canadiens.

The "Legion of Doom" carried the Flyers to the Stanley Cup Finals, falling in four games to the Detroit Red Wings.

2005—Perhaps the franchise's greatest non-championship team, the 2004–05 Eagles, had finally broken through and made it to the Super Bowl.

Behind a 13-1 start to the regular season (they finished 13-3 after resting key starters in the final two games), the Birds played in their first Super Bowl since 1980, after four straight cracks at the NFC Championship.

Two things resonate from the Birds' 24-21 loss to the New England Patriots: Terrell Owens' nine catches for 122 yards after a seven-week absence nursing a broken ankle, and Donovan McNabb's *did he or didn't he* on-field regurgitation (too much Chunky Soup?—see June 26th).

The Birds had a brief lead at 7-0, and were tied at half-time. But the New England offensive attack was relentless, asserting an effective ground game that the Eagles simply couldn't match. With 17 seconds remaining, McNabb was intercepted and the Eagles were sunk.

COLOR COMMENTARY

Like many other painful Philadelphia sports memories, this one ranks up there with the worst of them. I had just been hired by WIP as an update anchor and was just starting out in the media industry.

Although it was too late for a credential, I had decided to make the trip down to Jacksonville, sans tickets, with a few of my friends, joining the thousands of Eagles fans strutting the streets in full Eagles regalia.

As a fan my whole life, I was waiting for this day for a very long time.

It was a fun week, and despite the weather feeling more like Philly than Florida, it was a trip for the ages.

Luckily, two hours prior to kickoff, I finally scored a ticket for $1,900.00, and I was in.

What I recall is this: The Eagles were tied at seven at the half, but they should've been up by at least 14. Terrell Owens was the best player on the field. Andy Reid got outcoached. And I'm still trying to figure out what exactly happened in those last five minutes.

It's an awesome experience to see your team in the Super Bowl, but next time, I look forward to doing it without the terribly dejected flight home.

7th

1908—Philadelphia A's owner, Connie Mack, sold eventual Hall of Famer Rube Waddell, arguably the game's first eccentric madcap lefty.

Waddell was as famous for his womanizing, binge drinking, and reckless disregard (he once wrestled an alligator) as he was for his remarkable skills as a starting pitcher (2.16 lifetime ERA, ninth all time). Mack could no longer afford Waddell's baggage and sold his contract to the St. Louis Browns for $5,000.

WADDELL, ST. LOUIS AMER.

Waddell's 2.16 career ERA is 11th all time in MLB history (*Library of Congress*)

8th

1936—The NFL ran its first collegiate-player draft. It was the brain child of Eagles owner, Bert Bell, who suggested the "worst to first" selection style that we still see in the NFL today.

The first team on the clock? The Philadelphia Eagles, who selected running back Jay Berwanger, who would never play a down in the NFL.

A precursor to the J. D. Drew situation (see June 2nd), Berwanger made clear his intentions to never sign with Philadelphia, which forced Bell's hand in trading Berwanger to the Bears, as he had just won the Heisman Trophy with the University of Chicago.

Ultimately, Berwanger showed little interest in playing for *any* team. At the time, the college game was football's pinnacle, so Berwanger was content to sidestep the NFL for life as a foam rubber salesman and part-time coach at his alma mater.

He reportedly used his Heisman Trophy as the doorstop in his library.

Eagles coach/owner, Bert Bell, was elected to the Pro Football Hall of Fame in 1963.
(Philadelphia Eagles)

9th

1999—The Penn Quakers men's basketball team hosted the Princeton Tigers, who were coming off a nationally ranked 27-1 performance the season prior. By way of a 29-0 run by the Quakers, Princeton was down 29-3 early, with an impressive Ivy League win streak on the line. But the 33-9 Quaker lead at halftime turned into a stunning 50-49 Tiger win, as Princeton extended its winning streak against league opponents to 35.

Penn would get revenge, pummeling Princeton, 73-48, in the final game of the regular season, taking the Ivy League title and NCAA Tournament berth.

10th

1939—According to the Regatta archives, an organizational meeting at the Central Office of Eastern Intercollegiate Athletics on this date in 1939 developed the Dad Vail Rowing Association.

Named after University of Wisconsin-Madison rowing coach, Harry Emerson "Dad" Vail, the Dad Vail Regatta, brain child of Penn coach Rusty Callow, is the largest intercollegiate rowing event in the United States.

From its humble beginnings, as a four-school rowing event (Penn, Marietta College, Rutgers, and Manhattan College) that was part of an unnamed competition in 1934, the Dad Vail currently hosts over 100 schools, competing in about 150 races.

The annual event, which had called the Schuylkill River in Philadelphia home since 1953, was briefly seeking alternative sites for its 2010 schedule, due to diminishing funds.

The site got a stay of execution, however, with the Dad Vail inking a four-year agreement with Scottish Investment firm Aberdeen Asset Management, keeping the regatta in Philly through 2014.

As such, the event is currently known as the Aberdeen Dad Vail Regatta.

1949—The aptly named "Jumping" Joe Fulks, one of the pioneers of the modern jump shot (Philly's own Paul Arizin gets some recognition here too), and among the first NBA Hall of Fame inductees, scored a then-record 63 points for the Philadelphia Warriors in a 108-87 rout of the Indianapolis Jets.

11th

1995—The Flyers' short-but-sweet "Legion of Doom" line scored its first point in a 3-1 win over the New Jersey Devils.

After the dust settled on one of the most controversial trades in team history, the Flyers, sending their top-scorer Mark Recchi to the Canadiens for John LeClair, Eric Desjardins, and Gilbert Dionne, a potent offensive line emerged, dubbed "The Legion of Doom" by teammate Jim Montgomery. The invigorating youth and potential of the line, led by Eric Lindros, Mikael Renberg, and LeClair, was realized immediately.

Before the trade, the Flyers were 3-7-1 in the Atlantic Division standings, and after, they went 25-9-3, finishing in first place (28-16-4) in the strike-shortened year.

The trio survived three years together before Renberg's injuries made him expendable (in a deal that eventually landed Flyers great Simon Gagne in Philadelphia), with Lindros and LeClair delivering their best statistical seasons while part of the "Legion of Doom."

COLOR COMMENTARY

Out of all the years following the Flyers, there have been three lines that have been ingrained in the fans' memories. The first was the LCB line, with Hall of Famers Bobby Clarke and Bill Barber skating along with Reggie Leach. They were dominant and won a cup together. The second was the Crazy 8s with Eric Lindros, Mark Recchi, and Brent Fedyk. They were productive during a rebuilding time for the Flyers. The last was the Legion of Doom. They were big, strong, powerful, and at times, unstoppable!

In three regular seasons together, they combined for 305 goals and 361 assists, totaling 666 points. Eerie, huh? Just think of the totals they could've reached, without the extensive injuries costing them 301 games. Looking back at those great seasons in the mid '90s, it's amazing they didn't win a cup, as the closest they got was in 1997, when they were swept in the finals by Detroit.

Nonetheless, it was a great line that left a lasting legacy in the history of the Orange & Black.

12th

1930—Athletics owner/manager Connie Mack (officially, Cornelius McGillicuddy) won the prestigious Edward W. Bok Prize (known as the Philadelphia Award then after), given to the Philadelphia citizen who "during the preceding

Mack's "Mr. Baseball" statue, outside the Phillies' Citizens Bank Park (*Michael Kirk*)

year, acted and served on behalf of the best interests of the community."

Mack, who led the A's to a World Series victory in 1929, was the first Philly sports figure to win the prize.

13th

1981—"Linda 'HawkEye' Page is a one-in-a-million player," said Murrell Dobbins Tech girls basketball coach Tony Coma. "She's a Wilt Chamberlain to the girls' game."

On this day in '81—Friday the 13th, no less—Lady Mustang's Linda Page scored 100 points in a 131-37 drubbing of Jules Mastbaum Tech. She shot 41-for-58 from the field (a tad better than Wilt's 36-for-63 100-pointer in the pros) and 18-for-21 from the free throw line, with 19 rebounds, five assists, and seven steals in a game that only 53 spectators witnessed.

Page's individual achievement, while surely a well-earned feather in the sharpshooter's sweatband, was more a triumphant achievement for girls athletics overall.

COLOR COMMENTARY
(Ted Silary, *Philadelphia Daily News*)

Perhaps the coolest part of all this for Page was accepting a quick invite to zip down to the Spectrum for that night's Sixers game. She was introduced to the crowd, standing next to Julius Erving. And the next day's *Daily News* ran this headline, following a loss to Washington, across the top of the back cover: "Sixers Could've Used Page." The original intent that day had been to make sure Page would surpass 2,000 career points. She began with 1,963. But when Page finished the first half with 53, coach Tony Coma huddled the girls and mentioned Linda would need only 38 more to surpass

Wilt Chamberlain's 90-point barrier. He also said he was sure they would like to someday say how proud they were to play in such a special game. Did they resist? Not quite. As the players broke the huddle, they bellowed, "Break Wilt's Record!!"

14th

1977—Al Hill of the Flyers registered the best performance of his professional hockey career—in his first NHL game.

Having tallied two goals and three assists in the Flyers' 6-4 win over the St. Louis Blues, Hill set a league record for most points, with five (two goals and three assists), by a player in his first NHL contest.

A record-breaking career, however, was not in the cards for Hill, as the center would go on to score 40 NHL goals (all with the Flyers) in a career spent mostly in the AHL.

15th

1916—Sound familiar? The New York Yankees purchased the league's top home run hitter on this date after the player was stuck in a nasty contract dispute with his former team.

Famously, this is was what happened in 1919 when the Yanks acquired the great Babe Ruth from the Boston Red Sox. But the *poor man's* version actually occurred three years earlier, with Frank "Home Run" Baker.

Philadelphia A's owner Connie Mack, always the shrewd negotiator, sold the American League's four-time home run champ to New York after Baker had sat out the previous season over a payment discrepancy.

COLOR COMMENTARY

There's a reason Babe Ruth is regularly considered the game's greatest player. He made a guy named "Home Run" Baker look like a Little Leaguer.

Baker was leading the league in homers at a time when simply reaching double digits was an accomplishment. In 1921, his first season as a teammate of the Great Bambino, Baker hit nine home runs—which would have led the league in 1914. Ruth hit 59. Incredible.

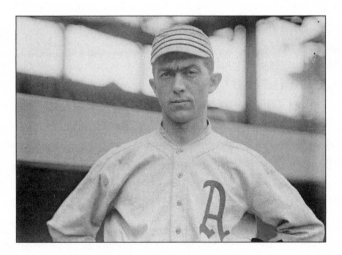

Baker, elected to the Hall of Fame in 1955, led the league in home runs for four straight years (1911–14) while with the A's (*Harris & Ewing*)

16th

1970—Philadelphia's most accomplished heavyweight, "Smokin' Joe" Frazier, won the undisputed title on this date, knocking out Jimmy Ellis in the fifth round at Madison Square Garden.

Ellis was little more than a space-filler, snatching up Muhammad Ali's vacated belt (draft evasion) in an elimination tournament of which Frazier refused to participate. Frazier's victory, while an important accomplishment for the champ, was essentially a warm-up for the "Fight of the Century" that would take place after Ali's reinstatement in '71 (see March 18th).

1985—The title of "largest crowd in NBA history" changed hands several times in the '80s, and the 76ers always seemed to have a piece of it.

In a 124-114 win over the Detroit Pistons at the Silverdome on this date, the attendance mark was set at 43,816. The two teams would break the record in '86 on February 15th (44,180), and again in '87 on February 14th (52,745). In '88, the Pistons chose a new partner, welcoming the Boston Celtics and 61,938 fans to the Silverdome, an attendance record that still stands today.

If All-Star games qualified, the 2010 midseason contest at Jerry Jones' Cowboys Stadium would have walloped the mark, with 108,713 mostly-squinting fans.

17th

1941—Gus Dorazio, punch-drunk fringe heavyweight contender, and possible inspiration for Sylvestor Stallone's

Rocky, lost his only title shot on this date (in front of a record 15,425 fans at Convention Hall) by a second-round KO against the legendary Joe Louis.

It was the signature fight for Dorazio, though his most notorious bouts came against the law. The most damaging punch the draft-dodger ever threw ended the life of Albert Blomeyer, and meant a second-degree murder charge for the troubled fighter.

1968—After a performance by the Ice Capades, strong winds blew part of the covering of the Spectrum roof off, forcing the Flyers to play their home games on neutral sites for the final month of the NHL season.

18th

1983—Who keeps track of these things? On a tip-in against the Houston Rockets, 76ers center Moses Malone tallied the NBA's four millionth point.

The nine millionth was scored by Portland's Juan Dixon in December 2005 against Philadelphia, and in January 2010, Ben Gordon of the Detroit Pistons scored the 10 millionth point, once again against the 76ers.

19th

2005—Bernard Hopkins became the first middleweight fighter in boxing history to complete 20 consecutive title defenses, earning a unanimous victory over European champ Howard Eastman.

Hopkins, age 40 at the time, accomplished the feat at an age when most fighters are long retired—and he's still at it today. His 20-plus-year reign in boxing is unparalleled in Philadelphia history.

20th

1997—In a 101-84 win over the LA Clippers, Sixers power forward Derrick Coleman scored 24 points and grabbed 20 total rebounds, to record a very rare 20-20 game. It would take six seasons for a 76er to match the feat, when Kenny Thomas dropped a 24-20 of his own on the Orlando Magic. Coleman, in his second tour with the team, scored 18 points with 13 rebounds in that game, for the second-to-last double-double of his career.

Both Chris Webber in 2005 and Samuel Dalembert in 2008/2010 joined the Sixers' 20-20 club.

21st

1978—On this date in '78, the West Philadelphia High School Speedboys basketball team lost to Overbrook, ending West's state-record 68-game winning streak. Spanning the 1976–78 seasons, the Speedboys streak was due in large part to the play of Gene Banks (class of '77), who would go on to win ACC Rookie of the Year honors with Duke, before a success-ful six-year NBA career.

COLOR COMMENTARY
(Ted Silary, *Philadelphia Daily News*)

My most vivid game memory on this one concerns the final few seconds. West's star player, Clarence "Eggy" Tillman, wound up with the ball at half court and had enough time to uncork a heave toward the south end of the gym. Instead, he momentarily froze, and did not cut loose until AFTER the buzzer, with 'Brook fans already storming the court. Our deadlines were ridiculously late in that era and I was asked to write a column at maybe 4 a.m. It was an incredibly busy day/night/morning. Gamp Pellegrini, who had coached St. Joseph's Prep to the football City Title a couple months earlier, resigned to become the head coach at Malvern Prep, so that was another big story to write.

1996—Losing 57-66 to the Miami Heat, the 76ers tallied the lowest point total in the franchise's 47-year history to that point.

What's more impressive—or depressive—is that Miami's 66-point total was the lowest single-game amount ever scored *against* the Sixers at the time (tied with Milwaukee in '55). In all, the 11,000 in paid attendance (the actual gate total was much less) saw the teams shoot a combined 35% from the field, while hitting just 3-for-32 from three-point range.

Just one of 64 losses for Philadelphia in 1995–96 (18-64), the Sixers' Conference-worst record was a necessary evil—it earned them the no. 1 pick in the NBA Draft, and the rights to take Allen Iverson.

COLOR COMMENTARY

The underappreciated bonus in the drafting of Allen Iverson was that, in taking over the point/shooting guard swing position, he replaced the man who had previously held the job—Vernon Maxwell.

Maxwell, who had been fined and suspended with Houston the season prior for fighting in the stands, had character issues that were no longer worth his competitive upside. He hit just one of 10 three-point attempts on this date, while shooting just 39% from the field on the season (didn't stop him from jacking up six three-pointers per game, though). The drafting of AI meant the end of the one-year Mad Max experiment.

22nd

1839—On this date in nineteenth-century Charleston, South Carolina, civil rights activist and baseball pioneer, Octavius Catto, was born.

One of the front-line leaders of the black baseball boom after the Civil War, Catto, co-founder of the Pennsylvania State Equal Rights League, formed the all-black Philadelphia Pythians baseball squad (see May 23rd) in 1867. He is credited (though nearly forgotten) as one of the catalysts for the popularity of baseball in the black community, back to its earliest roots.

Catto was assassinated on October 10th, 1871, at the age of 32.

This beautiful headstone was erected by the Octavius V. Catto Memorial Fund in 2010.
(*Michael Kirk*)

23rd

2005—The 76ers traded for Chris Webber. Then *both* proceeded to limp and hobble through the remaining years on his contract.

The trade, which sent Brian Skinner, Corliss Williamson, and Kenny Thomas to the Kings, and Webber, Matt Barnes, and Michael Bradley to the Sixers, was part of a series of missteps by the 76ers organization following the 2001 Eastern Conference Championship.

Thomas' seven-year deal with Philadelphia in 2003, worth $50 million, was perhaps the most damaging catalyst (see July 16th). With Thomas' production almost immediately in decline, the Sixers were all but forced to roll the dice.

Swapping bad contracts, the Sixers acquired Webber, bad knees and all, hoping he'd be the best of a bad situation. In the end, the Sixers had to buy out the remaining year and a half left on the pact, for $25 million in 2007.

Regrettable moves, compounded.

24th

1975—Recording artist Elton John released the hit single "Philadelphia Freedom," written by John for tennis star Billie Jean King and her fledgling World Team Tennis squad, the Philadelphia Freedoms.

John wrote the song after taking part in a promotional match during the league's inaugural season in 1974.

Currently featuring 11 teams nationwide, WTT is the country's only professional co-ed sport. King led the original Freedoms squad to the best record in 1974 before falling in the championship to the Denver Racquets.

25th

1972—The Phillies traded Rick Wise to the St. Louis Cardinals for Steve Carlton, in one of the greatest deals in team history.

Of course, Carlton went on to become the Phillies' most accomplished pitcher, holding the career strikeout record several times in a sparkling 329-win Hall of Fame career—but he wasn't exactly a diamond in the rough before coming to Philly.

Carlton was a key member of the St. Louis rotation for most of his seven seasons with the club, earning three All-Star bids before the trade. But because of a series of tense contract disputes over two seasons, Cards owner Gussie Busch demanded he be traded, and the Phillies, holding a disgruntled ace of their own in Rick Wise, happily obliged.

At the time, the deal seemed relatively even, as Carlton, 27, had won 20 games for St. Louis in 1971, and Wise, 26, had won 17 of his own—a no-hitter amongst them—for Philly. But in the end, Carlton would win 241 games for Philadelphia in his career, while Wise went just 32-28 in two seasons with the Cards.

Cards GM Bing Devine didn't see it coming.

"One's right-handed, and the other's left-handed," Devine insisted to the *St. Petersburg Times*, was the only difference between the two players.

26th

1968—With North Catholic High School's entire varsity basketball squad riding the bench as punishment for cutting class, coach Jack Friel led the junior varsity (!) squad to the biggest upset victory in Catholic League history, rolling Bishop McDevitt, 77-60 in the Quarterfinal. David had effectively *pummeled* Goliath.

North's JVs, who had managed just a split of the season series against McDevitt's junior varsity, played *way* up to the competition, behind junior Mike Kaiser's team-high 20 points. They had just a half-hour practice on short notice of varsity's suspension, and some players had to borrow sneakers before the team departed for the Palestra. But they managed, trailing just once in the playoff.

The story made national headlines, and the squad instantly cemented its status as one of Philadelphia's most unlikely underdog stories.

27th

1901—The National League Rules Committee changed the rules governing foul balls. Previously, a ball hit out of play had no effect on the ball-strike count, so players could foul off pitches without penalty to work the count in their favor. The rule instituted baseball's current system, which charges up to two strikes for foul balls.

More than any other Major League player, the Phillies' Roy Thomas, who once fouled off 27 pitches in a single at-bat, was credited with prompting the rule change. Thomas' pesky tactics led to a league-leading 115 walks in 1900.

28th

2008—Major League Soccer added its newest team, the Philadelphia Union. Based in Chester, the Union plays at its own PPL Park, built as part of a $77 million development and economic revitalization project.

Due to construction delays, the Union played its inaugural home game on April 10th, 2010 on more prominent grounds, the Eagles' Lincoln Financial Field.

A pro football game at the Linc in April—technically.

29th

1968—On a leap year, it's fitting to commemorate the season the Philadelphia Flyers leapt into the NHL with almost immediate success.

In a 3-1 loss to the LA Kings, Leon Rochefort became the first Flyers 20-goal scorer. Rochefort and the inaugural Flyers squad went a respectable 31-32-11 in their expansion

Rochefort (9), against the New York Rangers in 1968. *(Philadelphia Flyers)*

year, building toward a Stanley Cup Championship just six seasons later.

1980—Flyers great Simon Gagne, whose 259 goals with the Orange & Black are good for ninth in team history, was born on this date. In 2012, he celebrated his eighth birthday.

MARCH

1st

1938—Broad Street's The Blue Horizon, 2006 boxing Venue of the Year (*Wednesday Night Fights*, ESPN), ranked no. 1 (*The Ring Magazine*) and dubbed the "last great boxing venue in the country" (*Sports Illustrated*), housed its first professional bout. And it did so as the fraternal lodge #54 of the Loyal Order of Moose.

The Moose lodge didn't become "The Blue Horizon" until 1960, when boxing promoter Jimmy Toppi purchased the venue and began showcasing regular events there for the first time. Over the years, The Blue Horizon, with its rustic grassroots style, has ushered in greats such as George Benton, Bennie Briscoe, and Bernard Hopkins. Hopkins, "The Executioner," won his first professional bout at the venue in 1990.

(Michael Kirk)

Sadly, reportedly due to financial problems, The Blue Horizon was closed in 2010 and is scheduled for demolition to make room for hotel and restaurant development.

Did you know? Several fight sequences from the film Rocky V *were shot at The Blue Horizon.*

1999—In a 104-91 win over the Washington Wizards, 76ers coach Larry Brown tallied his 1,200th NBA game coached.

Just the 12th coach to do so at the time, Brown trailed only Pat Riley, Don Nelson, and Lenny Wilkens in games among active coaches.

2014—The 76ers retired Allen Iverson's No. 3 jersey in a ceremony at halftime of a game against the Washington Wizards. The 11-time All-Star and 2000-01 League MVP joined Hal Greer (No. 15), Billy Cunningham (No. 32), Bobby Jones (No. 24), Julius Irving (No. 6), Wilt Chamberlain (No. 13), Mo Cheeks (No. 10), and Charles Barkley (No. 34) in the rafters at Wells Fargo Center.

During his speech, in front of a sold-out crowd, Iverson said of his elite fraternity, "My name can now be mentioned with those names. Show me the fool who says dreams don't come true, because they do."

(Matt Rappa)

2nd

1861—Philly sports' first "eccentric" owner, Horace Fogel, was born in Macungie, Pennsylvania.

His ineptitude in professional baseball began as a manager, having been fired in 1902 after compiling a two-season record of 38-72 with New York. His final season with the Giants was cut short just in time—he had been trying out eventual Hall of Fame pitcher Christy Mathewson at first base.

Between 1902 and 1909, Fogel returned to sports writing, his original vocation, before taking over as part-owner and president of the Phillies.

His first order of business? Attempting a Phils name-change to the Philadelphia *Live Wires* (thankfully, it never materialized).

Fogel's stay in the Philadelphia limelight then ended abruptly in 1912, after Major League Baseball issued him a lifetime ban for repeatedly calling out league umpires for what he proposed were biased, unfair calls against his team.

Oddly enough, William Cox, Phillies owner in 1943, and Fogel are the only owners on MLB's lifetime banned list. Cox was banned for betting on his team's games.

1962—Wilt Chamberlain, with the Philadelphia Warriors, accomplished one of professional sports' most beloved individual accomplishments, scoring 100 points in a 169-147 win over the New York Knicks.

With starter Phil Jordon out with an injury, the Knicks used two backup centers, Darrall Imhoff, and the 6'6" Dave Budd, to oppose the mammoth 7'1" Chamberlain.

After The Big Dipper had scored his 79th point with just under eight minutes left to play, breaking his previous career high of 78, his Warriors teammates began feeding him the ball on every play.

At that point, what began as a typical NBA basketball game had become somewhat of a mockery. Reportedly, in the final minutes, the Knicks were fouling anyone with the ball except Chamberlain, to send his teammates to the foul line and change possession. To counter, Warriors coach Frank McGuire instructed his players to foul *back*, turning the final minutes into a 100-or-bust foul-fest.

In a game that Knicks guard Richie Guerin commented, "had nothing to do with basketball anymore," Chamberlain scored the final basket of his 100-pointer on a slam dunk (after two misses on the same possession) against a five-on-one defense, with all of his teammates left wide open.

The game was delayed nine minutes as fans at the Hershey Park Arena had rushed the court to congratulate

Chamberlain. While the game wasn't taped, the radio broadcast the game, and witnesses have suggested the last 46 seconds were played out. Harvey Pollack, longtime Director of Statistical Information for the Sixers and author of Chamberlain's scribbled "100" sheet from the infamous postgame photo, claims that Wilt stood idly at midcourt as time elapsed.

Initially, the game received only moderate attention, as media and fans had gotten used to Chamberlain's superhuman feats on the basketball court (Chamberlain himself called it "inevitable"). The initial lack of enthusiasm (and video replay), actually helped fuel the legend, as contradicting stories swirled, with game accounts varying from genuine to wild exaggeration. The 100-point footnote became the NBA's most storied regular season game.

Said Chamberlain later, in an ESPN interview, "I've probably had 10,000 people tell me they saw my 100-point game at Madison Square Garden. Well, the game was in Hershey and there were about 4,000 there. But that's fine. I have memories of the game and so do they, and over the years the memories get better."

Some side notes on the historic feat:

❖ The previous single-game record was 78 points, scored by Chamberlain against the LA Lakers three months earlier.
❖ The 316 combined points scored set an NBA record.
❖ The game served as a microcosm for two monumental *season-long* accomplishments in 1961–62, in which Chamberlain averaged an NBA record 50.4 points per game. And to speak, quite literally, of impossible feats, he also averaged 48.5 minutes per game that season, playing in 48 minute-long regulation games (the Warriors played

10 overtime games that season, and Chamberlain played nearly every minute of the season).

- ❖ Chamberlain's teammate, Guy Rodgers, recorded 20 assists.
- ❖ Warriors forward Paul Arizin scored just 16 points in this contest, but pitched a 100-point game of his own while at Villanova. The feat is not credited by the NCAA, however, as it was accomplished against a junior college.
- ❖ The contest also gave Chamberlain single-game records for most field goals attempted (63), field goals made (36), free throws made (28), and most points in a quarter (31) and half (59).

3rd

1983—Garnering a 23-11 record, winning his fourth and final National League Cy Young Award in his 11th season with the Phillies, Steve Carlton re-signed for four years and $4.15 million, making him the highest-paid pitcher in Major League Baseball history at the time.

COLOR COMMENTARY

Carlton seemed very conscious of the "highest paid" moniker. While most contracts in sports are backloaded, he had his frontloaded, with a $1.15 million year to start. Why? With Los Angeles Dodgers sensation Fernando Valenzuela getting a bump to $1 million,

Carlton would be number two to Valenzuela in salary for the 1983 season. Phillies president Bill Giles told the press he offered up the unique structure so that Carlton could "once in his life be the highest paid player in the game."

1993—Seven-feet, seven-inch center Manute Bol, the tallest player in 76ers history, sank six three-pointers in the second half of a game against the Suns.

Bol made just three three-point attempts through his first 239 career NBA games, but the conditions were right for the big man to break with conventions on this particular night.

The Sixers trailed 72-55 by the end of the first quarter, and head coach Doug Moe, out of desperation, gave Bol free reign from beyond the arc. His nearly flat-footed heaves, which included a windup that set the ball briefly behind his head, were ugly, but effective. Bol was 6-of-12 from three-point territory overall, helping Philadelphia outscore Phoenix in the second half, 60-53, though ultimately losing, 125-115.

4th

1944—Dig back far enough into Phillies history, and you'll discover their original (though unofficial) name was the *Quakers* until 1890. But, if you scroll through the team's 135+ years of history too quickly, you might miss their short-lived *third* installment in the nickname game—the Philadelphia Blue Jays.

On this date, the Phillies/Blue Jays adopted the new nickname as a way to cleanse the franchise from the stench of five straight 100-loss seasons and lifetime ban of team owner William Cox for betting on the team (the gambling debt alone should have been punishment enough). New owner Bob Carpenter held an open contest to select a new name for the squad, and "Blue Jays" (selected by fan Elizabeth Crooks) won, becoming the vaguely unofficial new moniker.

Not surprisingly, the idea began phasing out in 1945 and was scrubbed altogether by 1950, when Carpenter sold the team to a local syndicate.

History books sway on which to use (and Cox had actually failed with a similar move in '43, attempting to make the short-but-sweet "Phils" official), and the uniforms themselves were a bit confused. With "Phillies" across their chests, players adorned a Blue Jay patch on their left sleeve.

5th

2009—The Harlem Globetrotters, adding to their tremendous legacy, played their final game on the Wachovia Spectrum—that's right, *on*.

On this date, the near century-old basketball entertainment franchise played a rooftop exhibition game against its nemesis, the Washington Generals. The rivalry's first game at the site was *inside* the Spectrum, in 1967, the arena's inaugural year.

Where do they go from here?

Said showman, Kevin "Special K" Daley, "We might play on the moon next."

6th

1907—Former Phillies owners, A. J. Reach and John Rogers, were formally acquitted of damages resulting from the Baker Bowl bleacher collapse in 1903 (see August 8th) that killed

The Phils' new and improved bleachers of Baker Bowl, 1915 (*Bain News Service*)

12 fans and injured 232. Rogers, who bought Reach's ownership shares prior to the disaster, sold controlling interest in the team to James Potter in 1903.

7th

1993—Just 56 games into the season, the 76ers fired coach Doug Moe in his first season of a five-year pact with the team.

Today, Moe's short stint is the benchmark for ghastly Philadelphia coaching performances, as the team went just 19-37 under his tutelage. His conspicuous disregard for defense, while perhaps overlooked during his time with the high-scoring Denver Nuggets, ended his career when exposed with the post–Charles Barkley Sixers.

The team ended up at 26-56, surrendering 110.1 points per game, with coach Fred Carter at the helm to close out the season.

8th

1941—Hugh Mulcahy, a starter for the Phillies, became the first Major League Baseball player to be drafted into the armed services for World War II.

While his nickname—"Losing Pitcher" (which is just mean)—poked fun at his never having won more games than he lost in any of his nine Major League seasons (mostly due to playing for some pretty poor Phils teams), his bad luck streak did not extend overseas. Mulcahy passed away at the age of 88 in 2001.

1971—Billed "The Fight of the Century," boxing's top heavyweights squared off in a match that lived up to the hype, on this date at Madison Square Garden in New York City.

North Philly's own Smokin' Joe Frazier (26-0) took on Muhammad Ali (31-0) for the Undisputed Heavyweight Title, in a match that paired two undefeated legends, with opposing styles, from different backgrounds.

Ali, a public embodiment of the anti-war movement at the time, had just two re-seasoning bouts in 1970, after having his license revoked in 1967 for refusing to serve in Vietnam.

Frazier was a conservative supporter of the war and, combined with his trademark brawler style and punching power, found himself at natural odds with the conversely traditional, lightning-quick conscientious objector. It was Conservative vs. Liberal, and power vs. speed, with two undefeated fighters, fueled by more promotional hype than perhaps any other single sporting event in American sports history—and the fight itself didn't disappoint.

Relatively even after 10 rounds, Frazier pulled away, flooring Ali with a left hook in the 15th and final round, serving

Frazier compiled a 32-4-1 professional record, but, as an amateur, also secured a gold medal in the 1964 Summer Olympic Games. (*Nationaal Archief Fotocollectie Anefo*)

him just the third knockdown of his career. The tremendous blow punctuated a breathtaking unanimous victory for Frazier, handing Ali his first defeat, retaining the Undisputed Heavyweight Championship, and validating "The Fight of the Century."

9th

2002—Phillies skipper Larry Bowa earned the dubious honor of being suspended for a regular season game—while still in Spring Training.

On this date, Bowa's "inappropriate conduct toward the umpire," according to Major League Baseball, cost him an ejection from the Grapefruit League game, a one-game regular season suspension, and an undisclosed fine.

2000—The Harlem Globetrotters retired Wilt Chamberlain's no. 13 jersey during a show at Overbrook High in Philadelphia, Chamberlain's high school alma mater.

(World Telegram & Sun *photo by Fred Palumbo*)

Chamberlain, the first player to have his number retired with the Globetrotters, played for the traveling basketball showmen in place of his senior season at the University of Kansas. Due to NBA rules prohibiting players from competing without completing their final year of college, Chamberlain "settled" for a one-year, $50,000 contract with the Globetrotters (the average NBA salary at the time was $9,000, according to Robert Cherry, Wilt's biographer).

He played just the one season for the squad, completing a highly publicized tour of the USSR, and became a territorial draft pick of the NBA's Philadelphia Warriors in 1959.

10th

1980—The Lester Patrick Trophy was awarded to the Flyers' Ed Snider, Bobby Clarke, and Fred Shero, marking the first time a single team has had a player, coach, and executive awarded the trophy in the same year.

Honoring contributions to ice hockey in the United States, the fourth recipient of the award in 1980 was actually an entire *team*—the legendary 1980 US Olympic ice hockey squad.

11th

1986—The last time the Flyers and New Jersey Devils completed a player trade with each other, to date.

Dealing a third-round draft pick to Jersey, the Flyers received goaltender Glenn "Chico" Resch, a placeholder for incumbent Ron Hextall. Resch retired after the 1986–87 season, after 14 seasons in the NHL.

12th

1997—For a brief moment, Allen Iverson had bested Michael Jordan.

AI, enjoying his Rookie of the Year season, had one of his more recognizable moments in the NBA, baffling Michael Jordan with his signature ankle-breaking cross-over to sink a contested shot from the top of the key. Though the shot was irrelevant in the Sixers' 108-104 loss to the eventual 69-13 NBA Champion Bulls, Iverson had his moment, and Philly fans had hope (however fleeting).

It makes for a nice YouTube clip, as well.

13th

2005—Typically, one would not associate the play of Donyell Marshall with Kobe Bryant's exceptional game, but on this night, the two would share an impressive NBA mark.

Marshall (not yet a 76er), of the Toronto Raptors, tied Bryant's record of 12 three-pointers made, in a 128-110 drubbing of the 76ers. All but two of his game-high 38 points were threes, as Marshall hoisted a remarkable 19 shots from beyond the arc.

2015—On the first day of the official NFL year, Eagles Head Coach and General Manager Chip Kelly did the unthinkable (again)—he traded starting quarterback Nick Foles, a 2015 4th round pick, and a 2016 2nd round pick to the St. Louis Rams for the injury-prone former Heisman Trophy winner quarterback Sam Bradford and a 2015 5th round draft pick.

This surprising move was coupled with Kelly's decision to jettison franchise running back LeSean McCoy to Buffalo in exchange for Bills linebacker Kiko Alonso, yet another oft-injured and former Oregon Duck. Kelly seemingly needed salary cap space to make room for the subsequent signings of free agent running backs DeMarco Murray from the rival Dallas Cowboys and Ryan Matthews, formerly of the San Diego Chargers. Murray signed a five-year, $42 million contract, and Matthews was inked for three.

14th

1981—St. Joseph's men's basketball team, a no. 9 seed in the then-48-team NCAA tournament, defeated the no. 1 seed DePaul Blue Demons on a remarkable last-second layup.

Down 48-47, Hawks freshman Lonnie McFarlan, already mid–jump shot, found fellow frosh John Smith under the basket and unguarded. Smith landed a quick layup with two seconds remaining in the game to steal a 49-48 victory for St. Joe's in a tumultuous second round of NCAA tournament action.

Along with DePaul, no. 1 Oregon St. and the defending national champion Louisville Cardinals both suffered losses in the final seconds of play on this day.

1995—Dana Barros' 50 points on this night is as forgettable as a 50-pointer can be. Headlining the dilapidated Sixers squads of the post-Barkley/pre-Iverson era, Barros' feat came in a *29-point loss* to the Houston Rockets, 136-107.

Barros sank an impressive 21 of 26 field goals in the contest, while his team sank further into oblivion.

15th

2001—The Flyers inducted arguably their greatest defenseman, Mark Howe, into the team's Hall of Fame.

The franchise leader among defensemen in goals (138) and assists (342), Howe was a three-time First Team All-Star with the Orange & Black, and four-time winner of the Barry Ashbee Trophy as the Flyers' "most outstanding defenseman."

Howe was elected to the Hockey Hall of Fame in 2011. (*Philadelphia Flyers*)

16th

2000—Bob Clarke, commenting on his favorite topic—Eric Lindros—had, arguably, his biggest media blowup as GM of the Flyers.

With rumors swirling about the mishandling of Lindros' latest concussion after a March 4th game at Boston, Clarke took exception and went on the offensive during an impromptu televised mid-game interview.

"Don't just make stuff up and put it in the paper," barked Clarke toward a *Philadelphia Inquirer* beat writer. "You just make all this stuff up and write it as the truth. Talk to Eric. Talk to the trainers."

When the writer insisted Clarke wouldn't let him talk to trainers, the oft-candid Clarke uttered a live-TV no-no.

"Sure I do. They just won't talk to you, because you're an a**hole."

17th

1995—It was an unlucky St. Patrick's Day for the Villanova Wildcats men's basketball team. Having defeated UConn in the Big East Championship, and earning a coveted no. 3 seed in the NCAA Tournament, the Wildcats dropped the opening game in triple overtime to no. 14 seed Old Dominion, 89-81.

1997—The Eagles held a press conference to announce the signing of placekicker Chris Boniol. The 25-year-old Boniol had successfully made 59 of 64 field goal attempts the prior two seasons, plus two field goals for the Dallas Cowboys in their 27-17 victory over the Pittsburgh Steelers in Super Bowl XXX. It was downhill from there, though, as Boniol would finish his Philadelphia career after just two seasons, having hit only eight of 22 field goals of 40 yards or more.

18th

1991—The 76ers retired Wilt Chamberlain's jersey no. 13 before a 99-91 win over the Orlando Magic.

Chamberlain, the team's—if not the league's—most outstanding player, is one of eight players who have their jersey number hanging from the rafters of the Wells Fargo Center, including Allen Iverson (2013), Charles Barkley (2001), Mo Cheeks (1995), Julius Erving (1988), Bobby Jones (1986), Billy Cunningham (1976), and Hal Greer (1976).

Sharing the honor with the Golden State Warriors and LA Lakers, Chamberlain is the only player to have his number retired by three NBA teams.

2015—In a complete and mostly surprising move, Flyers General Manager Ron Hextall announced the hiring of Dave Hakstol to become the 19th coach in Flyers history. Hakstol, a college coach from North Dakota with zero NHL experience, replaced the fired Craig Berube.

19th

1967—With a 132-129 win over the Baltimore Bullets in the last game of the season, the 76ers had set the NBA record for wins in the regular season.

Comprised of future hall of famers Wilt Chamberlain, Billy Cunningham, and Hal Greer, the Sixers won 68 games (losing just 13, in yes, an 81-game season), an astonishing six

The 76ers, celebrating a championship season. (*AP Photo*)

more than the previous high of 62 set by the Boston Celtics two seasons prior.

Boston was, really, the lone thorn in Philadelphia's side in the 1966–67 regular season. Five of Philly's 13 losses came to Bill Russell's Celtics, which had played in the previous 11 NBA Finals.

The record was topped five years later by the LA Lakers (69-13), and currently belongs to the 1995–96 Chicago Bulls (72-10).

1981—Bobby Clarke scored his 1,000th NHL point, in a 5-3 Flyers win over the Boston Bruins at the Spectrum.

Bloodied from taking a slapshot to the head earlier in the game (remember, no helmets), Clarke's point came on an early third-period goal that gave the Flyers a 5-0 lead. At the time, Clarke was just the 15th player in NHL history to accomplish the feat—and the first to do it while wearing solely the Orange & Black.

On an added milestone note, Flyers great Tim Kerr registered his first career hat trick in the contest.

1996—Comcast announced its purchase of a 66% stake in the Flyers/76ers, and their two arenas. Of the remaining stake, Spectacor, headed by Ed Snider, took 32% of the venture, with the remaining 2% going to former Flyers team trainer and entrepreneur Pat Croce.

The 76ers were sold again in 2011 to an ownership group headed by private equity billionaire Joshua Harris.

2000—John Cheney's Temple Owls, the no. 2 seed in the NCAA Tournament, were bounced in the second round by Seton Hall, 67-65. Failing to match their Elite Eight performance in '99, which would have given Cheney his first Final Four appearance, the Owls, perhaps, missed the under-the-radar forgiveness of being a low-seed overachiever.

20th

1934—Olympic champion Babe Didrikson, no. 10 on ESPN's list of the top 100 North American athletes of the twentieth century, pitched a hitless first inning of an exhibition for the Philadelphia Athletics against the Brooklyn Dodgers.

So, what? Unlike Ruth, Babe Didrikson was female.

Founder and champion of the LPGA, All-American in track and basketball, and accomplished bowler, Didrikson—born Mildred—earned her nickname as a child due to her *Ruthian* home run blasts in schoolyard ball games.

Didrikson, with the St. Louis Cardinals, pitched her second and final inning of Major League Baseball two days after the feat, surrendering three runs to the Boston Red Sox.

1958—The Phillies acquired first baseman Joe Collins from the Yankees. Collins' reply? "If I can't be a Yankee, I'm through with baseball."

True to his word, Collins never played another game, nullifying the trade and starting a nasty trend of players refusing to report to Philadelphia, an act matched by Curt Flood after a trade from St. Louis ten years later (see October 7th) that would help establish modern-day free agency.

COLOR COMMENTARY

Hey Joe, Curt, J. D., and all the others who didn't have the desire or fortitude to play in our great city:
I think I speak for all Philadelphia sports fans when I say, "Who cares?"
In this city, if you don't want us, we don't want you, either.
Good riddance, and good luck—we don't easily forget.

1968—After a 137-119 win over the Baltimore Bullets the last game of the season, Wilt Chamberlain of the 76ers recorded a feat no other center in NBA history has ever accomplished—he led the league in assists.

Taking the cue from coach Alex Hannum, Chamberlain had adopted a more passive team-oriented style the season prior, failing to lead the league in scoring for the first time, but still finishing tops in rebounds per game (24.2) and third in assists per game (7.8). The strategy, meant to spread the offense while maximizing Chamberlain's vast array of talents, helped the Sixers win their first championship in 1966–67. In 1967–68, Chamberlain took the strategy to new heights.

Recording 702 assists (8.6 per game), Chamberlain had another record on his tremendous NBA resume, but failed to get past the Boston Celtics in the Conference Finals for the third time in four seasons. Individually, it was an all-time great season (Chamberlain himself had credited it as one of his finest accomplishments), but the team was left unsatisfied.

Traded in the offseason, Chamberlain played his last regular season game in a Sixers uniform on this date.

21st

1982—Andrew Toney set a Spectrum record for points in a quarter, scoring 25 in the fourth quarter of a 123-111 loss to the Boston Celtics.

Toney, known as the "Boston Strangler" for his many beantown beat-downs, too often gets overlooked as a crucial cog in the Sixers' championship run of the early '80s. The reason? Teammates and injuries.

Ankle and foot injuries ultimately limited him to just five significant seasons in the NBA, so his entire body of work is relegated to a short time period, in the shadow of his teammates' lofty career accomplishments. The third, or fourth, fiddle on those early-'80s Sixers squads, Toney's legacy gets lost in the debris of Darryl Dawkins' broken backboards, blocked by Dr. J's colossal afro, and trumped by Moses Malone's mouth and muscle.

In an interview with WKNR ESPN Radio in Cleveland, former Boston GM Pat Williams quoted Celtics great Danny Ainge as saying at the time, "Not Magic [Johnson] or Dr. J, it's Andrew Toney that keeps me awake at night!"

2015—The No. 1 seeded Villanova men's basketball team lost a heartbreaker to N.C. State, 71-68, in the NCAA Tournament's Round of 32. The Wildcats opened the tournament with a lights-out 63 percent shooting performance against Lafayette, but then shot just 31 percent from the field against N.C. State.

The disappointing loss continued a nasty trend of early exits for Nova, dropping their record to 3-5 in their last five NCAA Tournament appearances.

22nd

1960—The Philadelphia Warriors and Boston Celtics set an NBA playoff record on this date in '60, combining for 169 rebounds in the Warriors' 128-107 win in Game 5 of the Eastern Division Finals.

1984—Seven different Flyers scored, including hat tricks from both Ilkka Sinisalo and Dave Poulin, in a 13-4 win over the Pittsburgh Penguins that set a team record for goals in a single contest.

    The record, tied just seven months later in a 13-2 win over the Vancouver Canucks, still stands today.

1994—In his second tour of duty with Philadelphia, Moses Malone passed Elvin Hayes for third place on the NBA's all-time scoring list (currently seventh), hitting a foul shot to record his 27,314th point in a 91-125 loss to the Charlotte Hornets.

23rd

1979—The 76ers defeated the New Jersey Nets, 137-133, in double overtime on November 8th, 1978. On this day, the teams had a do-over.

    Protesting the loss because of too many technical foul free throws (four in all) being awarded to the Sixers, New Jersey was given a make-up game versus Philadelphia from the point of the first illegal technical—with 5:50 remaining in the third quarter.

    If that wasn't peculiar enough, during the lengthy layover between contests, the Nets and Sixers had completed a trade, with Eric Money and Al Skinner going to Philadelphia and Harvey Catchings and Ralph Simpson ending up in New Jersey.

After the re-do game, the box score featured Money's 23 points for the Nets . . . and four points for the 76ers, in the same game.

The Sixers once again were victorious, 123-117.

24th

1979—The Penn Quakers met the Michigan State Spartans in the Final Four of the Men's College Basketball Tournament.

Penn won its eighth Ivy League title in ten years, but the NCAA Tournament was a different machine altogether. Although Penn was once a powerhouse in Men's Basketball, as early adopters of the game from the late 1800s through 1920s, it was overmatched in a modern, NCAA Division I tournament format—with the Quakers' 1979 effort being the lone exception.

No Ivy League team has ever won the tournament, so Penn's Final Four game against Michigan State was an accomplishment that far overshadowed its 101-67 loss to the Magic Johnson–led Spartans squad.

The magical run, with wins over Iona, top-seeded North Carolina, Syracuse, and St. Johns, gave Penn its second Sweet Sixteen berth (1971), and first Final Four in team history.

COLOR COMMENTARY

Let it forever be said that "getting close" counts in horseshoes, hand grenades, and Ivy League team success in the NCAA Men's Basketball tournament.

25th

1981—On this date, the Phillies swapped broadcasters with the Atlanta Braves—sort of.

When the Phillies traded rookie and former third round draft pick Bob Walk to the Braves for Gary Matthews, they got more than just three years of playing service from the colorful five-tool outfielder.

"Sarge" Matthews went on to become a television broadcaster for the Phils while Walk, a ten-year veteran of the Pittsburgh Pirates after a trade from Atlanta in '83, is the longtime color analyst for Pittsburgh.

2005—In the Sweet Sixteen of the NCAA Tournament, the Villanova Wildcats fell to the North Carolina Tar Heels, 67-66—but not without controversy.

With his team down three points late in the game, Villanova's Allan Ray was called for a travel, negating a layup that might otherwise have been followed by a game-tying foul shot. The unsubstantiated call (check the replay) killed the Villanova comeback and launched the Tar Heels further toward an eventual National Championship.

26th

1991—Aiming for a heckler, Charles Barkley of the 76ers spit in the direction of the New Jersey Nets crowd. Misguided, in both thought and expectoration, Barkley ended up hitting an eight-year-old female spectator. Barkley was fined, suspended, and (perhaps unrelated) gone from the team a season later.

27th

2004—John Lucas III, of Oklahoma State, sunk St. Joes' dream season, nailing a three pointer to take the lead and eventual win (64-62) with 6.9 seconds remaining in the regional round of the NCAA Tournament. Led by the best guard tandem in college basketball in Jameer Nelson and Delonte West, the St. Joseph's University Hawks held the no. 1 ranking at regular season's end.

28th

1992—*College Basketball's greatest game ever played.*

The brilliant Elite Eight NCAA Tournament game highlighted by "The Shot" by Duke's Christian Laettner, against Kentucky in overtime with time expiring, was perhaps College Basketball's finest moment.

It helped cement a dynasty and perennial powerhouse in the Duke Blue Devils Men's Basketball team, and serves as the epitome of excellence and excitement in both the NCAA tournament and collegiate athletics as a whole.

Duke defeated Kentucky, 104-103, and took home the national title after wins over Indiana (81-78) and Michigan (71-51), respectively.

And it happened at the Spectrum in Philadelphia.

1999—Wrestlemania, pro wrestling's premiere event, was held in Philadelphia for the first time, at the First Union (Wells Fargo) Center.

The original event, held in 1985 at Madison Square Garden, helped launch pro wrestling into mainstream pop culture. The two poster boys for the inaugural event? Hulk Hogan and Mr. T, both signed by promoter Vince McMahon, in part because of their wildly popular performances opposite Sylvester Stallone in Rocky III.

By 1999, pro wrestling was in the midst of a second major surge in popularity. The main event pitted "Stone Cold" Steve Austin, one of wrestling's iconic figures, against Dwayne "The Rock" Johnson, who would prove to be, like Hogan, one of its biggest crossover stars and is currently a major Hollywood tough guy.

Austin won the match to retain the world title.

29th

2010—The Washington Nationals announced the identity of the person who would throw out the ceremonial first pitch on Opening Day (April 5th) against the Phillies in Washington, D.C.—US President Barack Obama.

April 14th, 2010, marked the 100th anniversary of the inaugural Presidential first pitch—William Taft's heater at the Washington Senators opener in 1910.

COLOR COMMENTARY

Maybe it's the predominant image of President George W. Bush rocketing home a strike after 9/11 at Yankee Stadium, but the wild floater thrown by Obama (a b-ball guy, by trade) was downright ugly. Given the emotional intensity of the moment, GW's pitch was, and still is, goose bump worthy.

(*Mr. Schultz, courtesy of Wikimedia Commons*)

2014—In a move that shocked Philly fans everywhere, the Eagles released Desean Jackson, one of the most popular and productive wide receivers in franchise history.

The twenty-six year old was just two years into a five-year contract extension, and was coming off his best season as a pro, totaling 1,332 receiving yards.

What gives?

While the truth never seemed to officially surface, rumors that swirled through the media when the Eagles made the announcement ranged from Jackson's alleged insubordination to his alleged ties with LA gangs.

Jackson caught 56 passes for 1,169 yards for the rival Washington Redskins in 2014.

30th

2009—Its fourth year in existence, the Phillies celebrated their Paint the Town Red Week—the first time as defending World Champions—to commemorate the community service efforts of nine "local champions."

The Celebrating a City of Champions Press Conference featured the dyed-red Phillie Phanatic, Mayor Michael Nutter, and Phils broadcasters Tom McCarthy and Gary Matthews, recognizing local community service efforts.

31st

1998—The Phillies played the National League's longest scoreless opening day game, as the Mets' Alberto Castillo knocked in the winning run of a 14-inning 1-0 New York Mets win.

COLOR COMMENTARY

The Major League record is also a hard-luck Philly opener—a 15-inning 1-0 Philadelphia Athletics loss to the Washington Senators on April 13th, 1926.

I was at the game against the Mets, and I really don't know why.

We took a road trip, ten of us to Shea Stadium for the season opener. The lineup for the Phillies included

Doug Glanville, Gregg Jefferies, Rico Brogna, and Mike Lieberthal. They combined to go 2-for-23 that afternoon.

Oh, and Mark Lewis and Desi Relaford were the middle infielders, and Ruben Amaro got into the game to play some left field. Whoopee.

In what seemed to be an all-too-familiar result following Phillies baseball, the team wasted yet another outstanding pitching performance. This time, it was Curt Schilling's brilliant eight innings of two-hit ball.

Four hours and thirty-five minutes after the first pitch, it was mercifully over at last.

Not shockingly, the Phillies finished 31 games behind the Braves that year.

APRIL

1st

1985—The Villanova Wildcats defeated the top-seeded Georgetown Hoyas in the NCAA Men's Basketball National Championship game.

April Fool's? Actually, the truth is better than fiction.

The '85 tournament was the first of the 64-team format, so Villanova's road to glory was long and arduous. The Wildcats, an eighth-seed, beat Dayton, Michigan (no. 1 seed), Maryland, North Carolina (no. 2 seed), and Memphis (no. 2 seed) before meeting the Patrick Ewing–led Georgetown squad in the final. The rest was madness.

Ewing and the Hoyas had won it all the season prior, with imposing physicality that even spilled over onto the sideline, with 6'10" head coach John Thompson calling the shots. But with no shot clock (it was introduced in the tournament the following season), 'Nova coach Rollie Massimino ran the Hoya big men silly, controlling the tempo and biding time for open shots. The strategy led to just six missed Wildcat shots all game (hitting 78.6% from the field), including only a single misfire coming in the second half. The 66-64 victory shocked the college basketball world and gave Villanova some staying power in NCAA lore, as the lowest seed to date to win the title.

1997—On this day in 1997, the Phillies' prized free agent signing, Danny Tartabull, was struck in the foot by an errant pitch. He was out of the game after just two at-bats. After a brief comeback attempt the following week, Tartabull was placed on the disabled list—for life.

The 14-year Major League veteran hit 262 home runs in his All-Star career, but lasted just seven at-bats in a Phillies uniform.

2nd

1992—The Phillies acquired pitcher Curt Schilling in a trade with the Houston Astros for Jason Grimsley.

Schilling, a member of the 10-man All-Vet Stadium team, pitched for nine years in Philadelphia, making three All-Star teams.

Grimsley never pitched in a single game for Houston, and won just 37 games over the rest of his career.

3rd

1901—Give credit to Connie Mack for knowing a good thing when he sees it.

Despite his best efforts, Connie Mack was never able to lure the PA-native, Christy Mathewson, to the A's. (*Bain News Service*)

On this date in Philadelphia Athletics history, Mack, the team owner, accused second-year (and future Hall of Fame) pitcher Christy Mathewson of reneging on a deal that would have resulted in Mathewson leaving the New York Giants for his A's.

In the end, Mack dropped the accusation, and Mathewson would collect all but one of his 373 career wins with the Giants (the last "W" came in a farewell stint with Cincinnati).

1987—In his last game against his former team, the Sixers' Julius Erving had his no. 32 Nets ABA jersey retired in a pre-game ceremony in front of 20,149 fans at the Brendan Byrne Arena.

In the 113-109 76ers loss, Dr. J had one of his worst shooting nights of the season, hitting just 2-for-12 from the field for six points.

His no. 6 Sixers jersey would be retired a year later, before a game against the Milwaukee Bucks, on April 19, 1988.

1989—Pete Rose was officially outted by *Sports Illustrated* for his baseball gambling misdeeds. The leader of the Phils' 1980 championship team did not fully admit to the accusations until 2004.

His lifetime ban from Major League Baseball has yet to be lifted.

4th

1941—This was perhaps the only time in sports history that two franchises traded *cities*.

Alexis Thompson, a young heir to a steel industry fortune, was turned down by Eagles owner Bert Bell to buy the Philadelphia franchise straight up. In a money-making opportunity, Thompson overpaid Steelers owner Art Rooney for the Pittsburgh franchise ($160,000 in all), and then Rooney pocketed half of the money after buying a stake in the Eagles from Bell. With that, Thompson aimed to move his "Pittsburgh Ironmen" to Boston, and Rooney/Bell aimed to claim all of Pennsylvania as their own—their home games being split between Pittsburgh and Philly.

Got all that? Problem is, other owners weren't too keen on Rooney/Bell's home *state* advantage, and Rooney was reportedly having second thoughts on bailing on his hometown franchise.

On this date in Philadelphia sports history, Rooney and Bell swapped *cities* with Thompson. Essentially, the Philadelphia Eagles became the Pittsburgh Steelers, and the Pittsburgh Steelers became the Philadelphia Eagles. Rooney got his hometown back, and Thompson got a franchise closer to his New York business holdings.

COLOR COMMENTARY

In case you find yourself questioning your Philly fandom, confusingly uncertain whether to root for the Eagles or Steelers now, no worries— the NFL defines a franchise's history by the city it occupies. So the Eagles you love is the same Eagles team now as it was before the big switcheroo went down. Bert Bell's pre-1941 Birds team is as much a part of Philadelphia Eagles history as the teams that followed. Even though, technically, the players on the teams that followed were Pittsburgh Steelers. I hope this helps . . .

1948—Athletics manager Connie Mack, 84, challenged Washington Senators owner Clark Griffith, 78, to a foot race from home plate to first base. The result? A tie. The real winners? The fans.

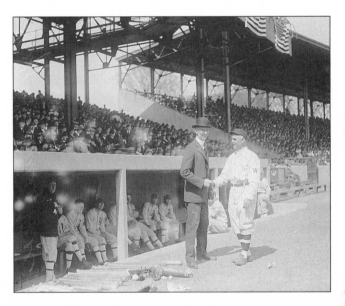

Mack, Griffith. Opening Day, 1919 (*Library of Congress*)

1971—Months away from their first game at the gargantuan concrete structure, the Phillies dedicated their new ballpark, Veterans Stadium, on this day in '71. The Philadelphia City Council chose the name to honor the veterans of all wars.

COLOR COMMENTARY

A sign of the times: The Astros' Enron Field (renamed Minute Maid Park following Enron's accounting fraud scandal) opened in Houston in 2000, and in 2009, the Mets unveiled their new digs, Citi Field.

The country's economic crisis of 2008–09 resulted in, reportedly, $45 billion in taxpayer funds doled out to Citigroup, as part of a major government bailout—raising eyebrows over the necessity (versus vanity) of Citigroup's $400 million naming-rights deal with the Mets.

Interestingly, if New York's City Council was awarded the same opportunity as Philadelphia's in '71, the Mets could currently be playing their home games in "Citi/Taxpayer Field," as such a proposal was brought before the council in November, 2008.

5th

1957—Long before Von Hayes earned the nickname "5-for-1" (see December 9th), there was another Phillie acquired at a five-player price who never quite lived up to the hype.

On this day in '57, the Phillies traded Ben Flowers, Mel Geho, Tim Harkness, Ron Negray, Elmer Valo, and $75,000 to Brooklyn for the lauded Cuban shortstop Chico Fernandez. His colorful name aside, Fernandez did little in his Phillies career to catch anyone's attention.

Over three seasons in Philadelphia and four more spent between Detroit and New York of the National League, the once-promising prospect earned a lifetime batting average of just .240, while once committing an abysmal 34 errors in a single season.

6th

2006—After a 4-2 loss to the St. Louis Cardinals, and an 0-for-4 day at the plate, Jimmy Rollins's hit streak ended at 38.

Challenging one of baseball's most cherished records—Joe DiMaggio's 56-game hit streak—Rollins's streak of 36 carried over from the '05 season. After going 1-for-4 in the first game of the '06 season, and 2-for-4 in the second, Rollins could do no more.

Since DiMaggio's streak in '41, only two players have gotten closer than Rollins (although Chase Utley lasted 35 games in 2006)—Pete Rose in 1978 (44) and Paul Moliter in 1987 (39). Just how remarkable is the record? DiMaggio's ironclad feat is 11 games better than the previous record (Willie Keeler, 45, 1896–97) and is widely considered one of professional sports' unbreakable marks.

1993—Whether he called the owner's bluff, yearned for greener (or Green Bay) pastures, or was simply not wanted, Reggie White, on this day in 1993, left Philadelphia to sign with the Green Bay Packers. The loss of the team's—and ultimately the league's—most prolific pass rusher was a heavy blow to the fan base, and proved costly to the team, as the Birds failed to top the .500 mark the following two seasons.

It was the final imprint left on the team by then-owner Norman Braman, whose stubborn refusal to concede to White's contract demands led one of the league's greatest defensive talents into a vast and conversely welcoming pool of NFL suitors.

7th

1984—Bobby Clarke played his last game in the NHL. This, his 1,280th game (including playoffs)—all with the Flyers—set a team record, going out with top Flyers marks in assists (852) and points (1,210) as well. But Clarke wasn't the only one saying goodbye.

After the Game 3 loss, 5-1 to the Washington Capitals, the Flyers team was also sent packing, having been swept in the Patrick Division Semifinals.

8th

1934—Philadelphia's first legal Sunday game between two Major League teams was played on this day at Shibe Park, between the Phillies and Athletics. The Phils won the hometown exhibition, 8-1.

Defeated the previous fall, Philadelphia's "Blue Laws" banned "unlawful gaming . . . disorderly sports and dissipation" on the Sabbath—not that it stopped Connie Mack from bending the rules eight years prior.

Though it was illegal at the time, A's owner Mack stubbornly fielded his team on a Sunday for the first time in 1926 in Philadelphia against the Chicago White Sox (see August 22nd).

9th

1913—In a 1-0 victory over the Dodgers, the Phillies took the win in the inaugural game at the iconic Ebbets Field in Brooklyn.

Other than housing the Dodgers until their move to Los Angeles in 1958, Ebbets Field was also an historically relevent football stadium. New York's first professional football team, the Brickley Giants (precursor to the modern-day Giants of NY), played the home games of its first and only season at Ebbets Field.

COLOR COMMENTARY

To this day, you can still catch a ballgame at Ebbets Field—provided someone's got the game on television at the current residence of 1720 Bedford Avenue—the Ebbets Field Apartments.

Genevieve Ebbets, daughter of Dodgers owner Charles Ebbets, throws out the first ball of the first exhibition at Ebbets Field, April 5, 1913 (*Bain News Service*)

10th

2000—The Phillies played their first home game in the 2000s. Actually, this date is commonly credited as either the first home game of the twenty-first century or first of the new millennium—but neither is correct, as '00 is the last year in a century and '01 is the first.

Either way, the 9-7 win over the New York Mets gave the Phils an exact .500 record in Opening Day games, at 58-58-2.

11th

1907—Who says only Philadelphia fans throw snowballs?

On this chilly April date, Giants fans at the Polo Grounds in New York unleashed a fury of snowballs in the wake of a poor home opener performance from the G-Men. When one got away and struck crew chief Bill Klem, the damage was done, and the Phillies were the winner by forfeit.

At the time the game was called, New York was trailing late, 3-0.

12th

1909—Shibe Park, the first stadium constructed from steel and concrete, opened in Philadelphia. Home of the Athletics, the park opened just five blocks west of the Phillies' Baker Bowl.

In 1938, the Phillies abandoned the Baker Bowl at midseason to share Shibe with the A's. When their American League counterpart bolted in 1954, the Phillies took sole possession of the park, at the time renamed Connie Mack Stadium.

Long lines outside Shibe during the A's 1911 championship season (*Library of Congress*)

2004—The Phillies, in another stadium first, hosted their inaugural regular season game at Citizens Bank Park, losing 4-1 to the Cincinnatti Reds. Built in part to give Philadelphia a stadium that would better equip the team to spend and compete with the top franchises in baseball, the Phillies delivered in 2008, winning the World Series on home turf. In 2010 the Phils set a team record for attendance (3,777,322), despite a seating capacity around 15,000 less than its previous home at Vet Stadium.

13th

1984—On the 21st anniversary of Pete Rose's first career hit, Charlie Hustle collected his 4,000th base knock, off Jerry Koosman of the Phillies, in the 5-1 Montreal Expos win.

Prior to the season, Phillies management granted Rose's release in hopes he'd re-sign and accept a limited role. Rose bolted for Canada instead, before going home again to Cincinnati at midseason.

Rose joined (and later surpassed) Ty Cobb in the elusive two-man 4,000 hit club.

2009—The Hall of Fame voice of the Phillies died of heart disease on this date in 2009. Harry Kalas, a tremendously popular TV and radio analyst for the Phils for almost 40

Sturmovik at en.wikipedia

years, actually began his broadcast career with the Houston Astros, from 1965–70. And while Philadelphia fans love (to mimic) Kalas' "Outta here!" home run call, his original signature longball catchphrase was, "That ball is in Astro orbit!"

COLOR COMMENTARY

It was perhaps the saddest day in Philadelphia sports history, and one of my most memorable in my media career. I was working in the WIP newsroom that day, delivering updates on the air when we got word that Harry passed in DC. I, along with an entire city, was just crushed. Devastated.

Harry Kalas was the soundtrack of our summers. The only baseball voice I ever knew in Philadelphia. He was one of the reasons I got into broadcasting. And here

I was, having to announce to the Delaware Valley that our beloved hero was gone. I led the report with "The Passing of a Legend" and trudged through that day with a heavy heart and misty eyes. It was very difficult performing my duties that afternoon. Kalas' voice was the narration of my childhood, the voice of baseball, and my friend.

Phillies baseball has never been the same.

14th

2000—In Game 2 of the opening round of the Stanley Cup Playoffs, Flyers winger John LeClair scored a series-turning goal—*through* the Buffalo Sabres net.

With his team down 1-0 at the time, LeClair fired a wrist shot toward the side of the net, manned by "The Dominator," Dominik Hasek. Unfortunately for Hasek and the Sabres, no one, including the officials, had noticed that the puck had actually gone *through* the outer part of the net and never actually crossed the goal plane (it is unknown whether the puck made, or simply took advantage of, the hole in the netting).

After the whistle blew on the game's restart, Sabres players tried to call attention to the hole, and protest the goal, but it was too late—a review cannot commence once play has resumed.

The Flyers won the game and, ultimately, the series.

15th

1965—With his team trailing 110-109 to the Boston Celtics with five seconds left in Game 7 of the Eastern Conference Finals, the 76ers' Hal Greer stood out of play, firing an inbounds pass in the direction of Wilt Chamberlain. Celtics broadcaster Johnny Most immediately made the "Sound-Bite Hall of Fame" with what happened next.

*"Havlicek steals it. Over to Sam Jones. **Havlicek stole the ball! It's all over! Havlicek stole the ball!**"*

Jones drained the remaining few seconds on the clock as Celtics fans stormed the court at the Boston Garden. The Celtics were on their way to their seventh straight championship season, as the Sixers had to settle for future promise.

Boston's eventual run of eight titles would end two seasons later, as the Sixers won their first title in Philly, capping off a then-record 68-13 regular season.

Havlicek, a familiar thorn in Philadelphia's side, won eight championships with the Celtics in his 16-year NBA career. *(AP Photo)*

16th

1953—Phillies second baseman Connie Ryan became the first and only player in franchise history to collect six hits in a single ballgame. Going 6-for-6 in the 14-12 loss to the Pirates, Ryan tied a then-MLB record for consecutive hits in a 9-inning game.

Pirates second baseman Rennie Stennett set a new benchmark in 1975, going 7-for-7 in a 22-0 pummeling of the Chicago Cubs.

1988—After finishing in first place in the Patrick Division the previous three seasons, the Flyers had uncharacteristically stumbled into the playoffs. They were 38-33-9 on the season, finishing in third place, facing the Washington Capitals as their first round opponent. On this day, the Flyers lost a heartbreaker in Game 7.

Having a stranglehold on the series, leading 3-1, the Flyers, led by defending playoff MVP and All-Star goaltender Ron Hextall, fell apart, losing the next two games to set up a deciding Game 7. Three regulation periods and an OT later, the Capitals (winning 4-3) were moving on, and the Flyers were sent packing. The final game was a fitting microcosm for the series—the Flyers had led the game 3-0 before Washington's comeback victory.

17th

1976—It's hard to upstage an 18-16, 10-inning win, after being down to the Cubs 12-1 in the early stages, but Mike Schmidt and the Phillies did just that.

Smacking four home runs in the contest, Schmidt tied the Major League record for home runs in a game, and became the third Phillie to accomplish the feat, joining Ed Delahanty and Chuck Klein.

A decade later, he'd bomb another benchmark . . .

1999—With the second overall pick in the 1999 NFL Draft, the Philadelphia Eagles selected Donovan McNabb ("Boooo!")...

Always a lightning rod for criticism during his long tenure in Philadelphia, McNabb garnered six Pro Bowl nods under center in the City of Brotherly Love.

But on this day, a select group of attending Eagles fans booed their disapproval—not so much of McNabb, but of the lost opportunity to draft upcoming phenom running back, Ricky Williams.

18th

1987—"Swing and a long drive, there it is, number 500! The career 500th home run for Michael Jack Schmidt!" exclaimed an exulted Harry Kalas as "Michael Jack" touched em' all for the career milestone. What gets lost in the career accomplishment however, is that the home run, coming in the top half of the ninth inning with two outs, gave the Phillies the lead, and the win, 8-6 over the Pittsburgh Pirates.

Hitting 548 home runs in all, Schmidt was hardly a one-trick pony. His 18-year career, all in Philadelphia, included 12 All-Star selections, 10 Gold Gloves, and three league MVPs. His stoic, business-like approach on the diamond made him an easy target for frustrated fans at times, but both his bat

COLOR COMMENTARY

Schmidt hit 548 home runs in his career and this, obviously, was the signature swat of them all. I was watching the game on television and remembering it being a sunny afternoon in Pittsburgh. Growing up watching the Phils was tough, and even though they weren't very good back then, it was always fun watching Michael Jack come to the plate.

I'll always remember him slapping his hands and celebrating down the first base line, the cut-aways to his proud wife Donna in the stands, but mostly the absolute thrill and happiness in Harry Kalas' voice. He loved calling Schmitty's home runs, and this one was probably one of his best calls of all time. "There it is, number 500..."

and glove work at third base were prodigious enough to excuse his frequent lack of enthusiasm.

19th

1900—The Phillies beat the Boston Beaneaters, 19-17, in Major League Baseball's highest-scoring Opening Day game to date.

1997—The Philadelphia Phantoms, of the American Hockey League (AHL), played their first Calder Cup playoff game, a 4-2 win over the Baltimore Bandits.

A developmental affiliate of the Flyers, the short-lived Phantoms of Philly (operating from 1996–2009) were as quick to collect championships as the Flyers were in their early expansion years. The Phantoms won the Calder Cup in 1998 and 2005, before being moved to Glen Falls, NY, in 2009.

In 2014–15, the current *Adirondack* Phantoms will return to the Philadelphia area, in their brand new home in Allentown, PA.

Also, the Flyers played a game of their own on this date, picking up the second leg of the Corestates (Wells Fargo) Center double header, defeating the Pittsburgh Penguins, 3-2, in Game 2 of the Eastern Conference Quarterfinals. At the time, the 19,812 fans in attendance made up the largest crowd in Flyers history.

20th

2003—Maybe he was not that big a player in *practice*, but Allen Iverson was surely a postseason gem for the 76ers.

On this date, the first game of the 2003 playoffs, AI dropped 55 points on the New Orleans Hornets, on 21-for-32 shooting, in a 98-90 win.

At the time, Iverson was just the sixth player in NBA history to score at least 55 in a playoff game.

Wilt Chamberlain, Rick Barry, Elgin Baylor, Michael Jordan (five times, but who's counting?), and Charles Barkley were the others.

2015—The Eagles signed veteran Tim Tebow, the immensely popular 2007 Heisman Trophy-winning quarterback, who hadn't previously thrown a pass in the NFL since 2012.

Tebow seemingly outplayed then-third-string quarterback Matt Barkley in the preseason, but head coach Chip

Kelly elected to proceed without either quarterback, trading Barkley before the start of the season on September 4, and releasing Tebow the following day.

21st

1895—The longest uninterrupted collegiate track meet in the country began on this date. In part, Philly's own Penn Relays served as an introduction to the University of Pennsylvania's new stadium, Franklin Field.

The first meet featured nine relay events—four for high school, four for college, and a collegiate championship—and Harvard took the inaugural title (4x400 yards) over Penn.

Currently, there are over 300 events, and 22,000 participants. According to competition officials, more athletes have run at the Penn Relays' 115 annual installments than at any other single meet in the world.

1991—In one of the more regrettable moves in team history, the Eagles traded 1991 and 1992 first-round picks to Green Bay for the draft rights to offensive tackle Antone Davis, who, after a seven-year NFL career, never lived up to the high price tag.

Ironically, the Eagles lucked out a bit in losing their '92 selection. In a relatively weak first round, the Birds, who would have picked fifth, might have selected Troy Vincent, who went seventh to Miami before eventually earning five Pro Bowl appearances for the Birds anyway.

1993—The Eagles knew they were attempting the impossible—replacing the departed Reggie White. On this date in history, they actually took a step backward in their retooling of the pass rushing unit, signing linebacker Tim Harris. Harris had recorded 17 sacks the season prior with the San

Francisco 49ers, but would see only four games of action in his Eagles career. After one season spent mostly on the injured reserve list, the Eagles nixed their three-year pact with Harris.

22nd

1957—John Kennedy made his Major League debut with the Phillies—John *Irvin* Kennedy.

A shade over ten years to the day that Jackie Robinson made his debut with the Brooklyn Dodgers, breaking the color barrier, the Phils put Kennedy in play, the franchise's first African American player. The Phillies, one of just three MLB teams to remain segregated after Robinson had *retired*, hadn't exactly forced the window of opportunity wide open—Kennedy's Major League career spanned just two at-bats.

As the following day's anniversary proves, it's not exactly the team's proudest of times . . .

23rd

1947/2007—Unfortunately for the Phillies, timing is everything. Because of a previous rain-out, the Phils pushed their scheduled "Jackie Robinson Day" to this date in 2007. What's the significance? While April 15th, 1947 marks the actual date of Robinson's breaking of the Major League color barrier, the following week (April 22nd–24th) marks the anniversary of perhaps the most vicious welcome Robinson ever encountered—from then-Phillies manager Ben Chapman.

Chapman, as adamantly opposed to the desegregation of baseball as anyone, did everything in his power to let Robinson know how he felt—from ordering intentional bean-balls, to spewing malicious banter toward Robinson from the dugout that, in this book, is surely unfit to print.

When the dust settled on the three-game series, Robinson had endured it all, and kept his cool. If any positives can be spun from the situation, it's that Chapman had made it easy for the public to cast a sympathetic eye toward Robinson. Chapman made himself the clear antagonist in this story, and Robinson, as always, was the quintessential American sports hero.

In the 2013 movie *42*, a Hollywood retelling of Jackie Robinson's successes and tribulations upon breaking baseball's color barrier, Alan Tudyk gives one of the film's most gut-wrenching performances in recreating Chapman's vile behavior.

Film critic Richard Roeper called it, "the most disturbing and, in some ways, the most important scene in *42*."

24th

1967—With a 125-122 win over the San Francisco Warriors in Game 6 of the NBA Finals, the 76ers had their first NBA championship (excluding the Nationals' '55 championship in Syracuse).

The team was stacked. Wilt Chamberlain, Billy Cunningham, and Hal Greer—three hall of famers all in their prime—led the Sixers to a league-record 68 wins. Jumping to a 3-0 series lead, they dismantled Bill Russell's Celtics in the

Conference Finals in just five games—setting up the first NBA Finals in 11 years not featuring Boston.

The San Francisco Warriors, the NBA pride of Philadelphia just five years prior, stood alone between the Sixers and their first championship.

Game 1 of the Finals was an overtime thriller, with the Sixers pulling it out, 141-135. Had they not won the game, the series might have played out differently. But as it was, it was business as usual for the '66–'67 Sixers, as Greer once boasted, "We knew we were going to win most of our games—it was just a matter of by how much."

A 126-95 Philadelphia drubbing in Game 2 notwithstanding, the Warriors posed the Sixers their first legitimate threat, but ultimately fell in Game 6 to arguably the greatest team ever assembled.

Said Wilt Chamberlain shortly before his death in 1999:

The best team I ever saw was the 1966–67 Philadelphia 76ers.

25th

1989—Mario Lemieux, of the Pittsburgh Penguins, registered one of the most dominant playoff performances against *any* professional Philadelphia team.

Lemieux scored four goals in the first period alone (an NHL playoff record), en route to a five-goal (another playoff record), three-assist performance. His eight points in the game were also a playoff a record.

The Flyers got the last laugh, though, winning the Patrick Divison Finals series, 4-3 (see April 29th).

26th

1959—Pitching in relief of a 9-2 Phillies loss to the Pittsburgh Pirates, Gene Conley, at 6'-8", became the tallest pitcher in franchise history. Conley was an All-Star that season, going 12-7 with a league-leading 136 ERA+.

1976—Mike Schmidt, with two bombs in a 10-9 win over the Cincinnati Reds, set a single-season Major League record with 11 home runs in the month of April (through the first 12 games).

Currently, Albert Pujols and Alex Rodriguez share the record, with 14 April homers.

1984—The 76ers, returning essentially the same team from their championship roster the season before, defined the "championship hangover." 52 regular season wins is nothing to scoff at, but it wasn't the dominant 65 posted the season prior. Shockingly, the Sixers fell to the New Jersey Nets in the first round of the playoffs, dropping the deciding Game 5 on this date, by a score of 101-98.

27th

2003—Kevin Millwood, a new addition to the Phillies rotation acquired from Atlanta, pitched the second of two no-hitters in Veterans Stadium history (Terry Mulholland, 1990). Centerfielder Ricky Ledee made the final out in the Phils' 4-0 victory over the San Francisco Giants.

COLOR COMMENTARY

Kevin Millwood will forever be remembered in this town as another one of those players who was always better somewhere else than he was in Philadelphia. But on this day, he was damn-near perfect, only allowing three walks while striking out 10.

Like many great sporting events, you tend to remember where you were when they occurred. If you care, I was outside on this sun-splashed April afternoon, installing a fence at my home. I spent the eighth and ninth innings inside my truck in the parking lot of Home Depot. I had to get a few items, but didn't go into the store for 40 minutes. I was enjoying Harry Kalas painting another vivid picture for me, taking me right to the Vet, as he had done all my life.

28th

1929—The Philadelphia Athletics won, 7-3, over the Red Sox in Boston's first-ever Sunday home game. Unlike Connie Mack's A's had done in their first holy-day game (see April 8th), Red Sox brass avoided the backlash of playing so close to a church's vicinity by hosting the game at Commonwealth Park (home of the Boston Braves).

29th

1989—The Flyers, at one time trailing 3-2 in the Patrick Division Finals, defeated the Pittsburgh Penguins in Game 7, 4-1.

The Fly Guys, an unlikely contender at 36-36-8 on the regular season, would lose the Conference Finals to the Montreal Canadiens in six games.

30th

1887—Departing the quaint Recreation Park, the Phillies opened a state-of-the-art stadium of their very own—National League Park—on this date in 1887.

The Park (eventually known as Baker Bowl, after owner William Baker), pioneered the brick exterior construction style that most new stadiums, including Citizens Bank Park, pay homage to today. The interior decorating, however, is what interested most National League hitters.

Baker Bowl was a classic bandbox, featuring a 40 ft. tall right field wall (with a 20 ft. screen extension added in 1915) just 280 feet from home plate—although it didn't always provide a strong home-field advantage. The Phillies finished higher than third place just six times in its 52-year tenancy at Baker Bowl.

Prime example: The 1930 Phils, slugging away at the then-deteriorating Baker Bowl, scored a franchise-record 944 runs while hitting .315 collectively. The team finished dead last.

And although the league as a whole hit an unfathomable .296 that season, Baker Bowl was still in a category all its own.

1919—Only two players in Phillies history have ever pitched the equivalent of two 9-inning ballgames in a single contest, and the last such occurrence was on this date, about 100 years ago.

Right-hander Joe Oeschger pitched all 20 innings in the Phillies' 9-9 tie against the Brooklyn Dodgers, one of 104 ties in team history. Oeschger matched the Phillies record for most innings pitched in a single contest, and is the only pitcher with two 20-inning outings in his career, having pitched an MLB-record 26 frames in 1920 for the Boston Braves.

Ever-durable, Oeschger, at 91 years old, threw out the first pitch at Veterans Stadium before Game 3 of the 1983 World Series.

1st

1998—Reality struck for the Flyers. A year after being swept by the Detroit Red Wings in the Stanley Cup Finals, the Flyers were ousted in five games in the first round by the Buffalo Sabres, 3-2. It wasn't their last shot at glory, but it was certainly the beginning of the end for a team built to win it all.

2nd

1908—The US Copyright Office received a copy of the song, "Take Me Out to the Ball Game," by Philadelphia's own singer/songwriter Jack Norworth.

Routinely played during the seventh-inning stretch of baseball games nationwide, Norworth's lasting hit was originally longer—the minute-long chorus is the simplified version we sing today.

Jack Norworth & Albert Von Tilzer

1999—In Game 6 of the opening round of the NHL Playoffs, the Toronto Maple Leafs defeated the Flyers 1-0 on a goal scored with 59 seconds remaining in regulation, taking the series, 4-2. Adding salt to the wound, Maple Leafs goaltender Curtis Joseph, rumored to have been favoring Philadelphia, was passed over in free agency the previous offseason by the Flyers. Joseph would make two consecutive All-Star appearances with Toronto, en route to a very successful 19-year NHL career.

3rd

1981—One of the greatest games, featuring two of the greatest teams, in one of the greatest series in NBA history took place on this day. The 76ers, blowing double-digit leads in both Games 5 and 6, watched a 3-1 Eastern Conference Finals lead turn to a winner-take-all Game 7 against the Boston Celtics. Continuing the trend of the previous two matchups, the Sixers' 11-point lead dissipated, as Larry Bird sank the game winner in the final minute, taking it for Boston, 91-90.

Not a great date in 76ers history...

2002—Another deciding playoff game against the Boston Celtics, another agonizing defeat. The 76ers rallied back from an 0-2 hole to draw even entering the final game of the opening round five-game series against Boston. The Sixers' luck would end there. Boston shot 66.7% from beyond the arc (9-for-10 in the fourth quarter), sending the defending Eastern Conference champs home early, 120-87.

4th

2004—The Flyers defeated the Toronto Maple Leafs, 5-4, in Game 6 of the Conference Semifinals, on a remarkable overtime goal by Jeremy Roenick.

The gritty leader of the Fly Guys hadn't scored in seven games, but came up big at the seven minute, 39 second mark of an overtime period super-charged with emotion.

Seconds before the clinching goal, Flyers winger Sami Kapanen was leveled by Toronto's Darcy Tucker, stumbling several times in his attempts to regain his balance and get back to the bench.

It was a heroic display of toughness by Kapanen, and an incredibly satisfying victory for the Flyers.

Ultimately, the Flyers would lose in seven games to the Tampa Bay Lightning, but it was games and series like this one that made the 2004 Flyers playoff run amongst the most exciting in recent team history.

COLOR COMMENTARY

As relayed in my book, *Flyer'd Up,* this game, still to this day, is my favorite Flyers game of all time!

I was in a NY hotel, away on business, and not yet working in the media. I still remember that overtime as some of the best end-to-end action I had ever seen. From the near misses just moments before the goal, to the brave Sami Kapanen staggering back to the bench after another cheap shot from Toronto's Darcy Tucker.

When Roenick came streaking down that right side on a two on one with Tony Amonte, I rose to my feet, threw my arms high into the air, and didn't stop smiling for the next 12 hours. That was one great night. Beers, wings, a Flyers win, yet another conference final appearance, and a victory cigar.

Roenick may have only played three seasons in Philadelphia, but his playing style, his honesty, his emotion, and this particular goal will have him holding down a piece of Flyers' history forever, and he will always be recognized as a fan favorite.

2000—Hmm, which day to choose? After all, the Flyers began play in this eventual quintuple-overtime game (yup, that's five) on May 4th, attempting to tie the Eastern Conference Semifinal series with the Pittsburgh Penguins at two games apiece . . .

(continued on May 5th)

5th

2000— . . . but ended at 2:35 AM EST on May 5th with one of the most cherished goals in Flyers history.

The six hour, 56 minute game set an NHL record for real-time elapsed, as both Philadelphia and Pittsburgh labored through four and a half overtimes of scoreless hockey, locked up at 1-1. Rookie goaltender Brian Boucher stopped 57 of 58 shots when it was all over, but the player of the game was a laboring Keith Primeau, who scored the game-winner.

Primeau whipped a wrist shot past the understandably weary goalie, Ron Tugnutt, to tie the series and set off one of the most dramatic and effective momentum-shifters in Philadelphia sports history. The Fly Guys would send the Penguins packing with relative ease in the next two games, winning the series in six games.

At its conclusion, Tugnutt summed up the marathon—
"People were starting to ask what period it was."

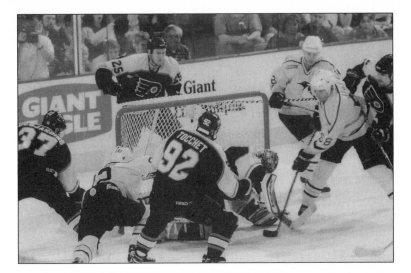

Primeau (25) arrived in early 2000 as part of a trade that sent away fan-favorite Rod Brind'Amour. He wasted little time in cementing his own Philly legacy. *(Philadelphia Flyers)*

2015—Making his Major League debut, Phillies reliever Elvis Araujo struck out two of the five batters he faced, in a scoreless 6th inning of a 9-0 loss to the Atlanta Braves.

Notably, at 270 pounds, Eraujo became the heaviest player in Phillies history. Of course, players' "official" weights are historically dubious, but Eraujo's is the highest on record. Former Phillie Carlos Silva ballooned to 280 pounds with Chicago at the end of his nine-year MLB career, but while a rookie with Philadelphia, Silva was just a svelte 225.

6th

1976—"The Riverton Rifle" Reggie Leach scored five goals in a Game 5 semifinals Flyers win over the Boston Bruins, 6-3. His postseason heroics in 1976 had the Flyers playing in their third straight Stanley Cup Finals.

Leach earned the Conn Smythe Trophy as the playoffs' MVP (in a losing Flyers effort), after setting a record for most goals in a single playoffs (19). This record was tied by Jari Kurri in 1985, but still stands today.

7th

2001—Construction began on the Eagles' new nest, Lincoln Financial Field, replacing Veterans Stadium, home of the Birds since 1971. Lincoln Financial Group purchased the naming rights in a 21-year, $139.6 million deal.

2002—Allen Iverson talked about practice. Not a game. Not a game. Not a *game*. He talked about practice.

By now, you've seen it. You've probably heard it parodied even, ad nauseam.

But what brought on Iverson's obsessive rant about *practice*?

Following an early playoff exit in 2002, a season removed from the NBA Finals, Coach Larry Brown had frequently questioned Iverson's practice habits in the press. When called out on it in a short press conference, Iverson went on to say the word "practice" 14 times.

"I know it's important," AI quipped about the p-word, "I honestly do, but we're talking about practice. We're talking about practice, man. We're talking about practice. We're talking about practice. We're not talking about the game. We're talking about practice. When you come to the arena, and you see me play, you've seen me play right, you've seen me give everything I've got, but we're talking about practice right now."

2014—The Philadelphia Flyers promoted Assistant General Manager Ron Hextall to general manager and moved current GM Paul Holmgren upstairs to be named team president. Hextall, one of the most beloved players in the history of the organization, gained valuable experience serving as assistant GM to Dean Lombardi in Los Angeles for seven seasons before returning to the same role with the orange and black in 2013.

8th

1980—In a Game 5 semifinal win (7-3) over the Minnesota North Stars, Bill Barber tied Reggie Leach's team record for goals in a single playoff series (see May 6th), netting his ninth. In addition, Barber set a new series team record for points (12) and, with a shorthanded goal in the game, the left winger became the only player in NHL history to score three shorthanded goals in a series.

With the win, the Flyers had won the series, 4-1, to advance to the Stanley Cup Finals.

9th

1937—In a brutal 21-10 Phillies loss to the Cincinnatti Reds at Baker Bowl, the Cincy catcher, Ernie Lombardi, tied the modern major league record of six hits in six consecutive at-bats.

Perhaps fittingly, Hugh "Losing Pitcher" Mulcahy took the big loss for the Fightins (see March 8th).

10th

1895—One of the game's original sluggers, the Phillies' Sam Thompson became just the third player in league history at

Then with the Detroit Wolverines, Sam Thompson poses for one of the first baseball card sets produced for tobacco promotion (*Library of Congress*)

the time to hit 100 career home runs, in a 14-4 victory over the St. Louis Browns. Currently, there are 25 members of the *500* home run club.

Thompson, elected to the Hall of Fame in 1974, was the game's first 20-20 player, slugging 20 homers and swiping 24 bases during the 1889 season.

11th

1986—It can be argued that this was the last day of the 76ers' reign among the elite of the NBA. It was Game 7 of the Eastern Conference semifinals, with the Sixers down by a single point, and the ball in Julius Erving's hands for one final play. The shot that followed—a wide open jumper from 15 feet out—meant more than just the difference between victory and defeat in a single contest or series.

Unknown to Dr. J at the time, the ball carried the weight of the franchise as it left his hands—perhaps just enough weight to clank it off the rim, ending the game (113-112 for the Milwaukee Bucks), and setting forth a chain of events that would drastically alter the course of the perennial East contenders. A month later, Moses Malone and the first overall pick were traded, and a return to the Conference Finals would begin an arduous 14-year journey.

12th

1910—Chief Bender, of the Philadelphia Athletics, hurled a near-perfect no-hitter, disposing of the Cleveland Naps, 4-0.

Chief, born Charles Albert, was half Chippewa Indian, and one of the first Native Americans to play in the Majors.

Bender, right, chatting up John "Chief" Meyers of the New York Giants during the 1911 World Series (*Bain News Service*)

Eight times in his career he won at least 16 games, finishing with a remarkable 2.46 ERA, though his wait for induction into the Hall of Fame would be nearly thirty years after his retirement.

2008—Outfielder Jayson Werth became just the second Phillies player in history to rack up four stolen bases in a single contest. His last was the most impressive, stealing home on Dodgers pitcher Ronald Belisario, en route to a 5-3 Phillies win.

Werth tied the record set in 1978 by Phillies great, Garry Maddox.

13th

1985—Construction began on One Liberty Place in Philadelphia, breaking longstanding tradition that no building would be made to eclipse William Penn's statue atop City Hall.

(*Carol M. Highsmith*)

Over time, the building's construction would be the instigator in the "Curse of Billy Penn" theory, to explain the 25-year professional championship draught in Philadelphia. In June 2007, a Penn statuette topped off the construction of the Comcast Center, currently the city's tallest building.

In 2008, the Phillies won just their second world championship.

Coincidence?

1999—In a 97-85 win over the Orlando Magic in the opening round of the playoffs, 76ers' guard Allen Iverson recorded 10 steals, a postseason league record.

AI added 33 points in the Game 3 win and helped seize the series in Game 4 (101-91) before the Sixers ultimately fell to the Indiana Pacers in the conference semifinals.

14th

1883—The Quakers (Phillies) won their first game, 12-1 over the Chicago White Stockings, and began their first winning streak (two games) as a pro franchise. It took the struggling upstart team nine games to achieve the victory, in a season that would prove to be its first and worst, going 17-81. The two-game winning streak remained a team record until the following season.

Contrary to popular belief, it wasn't all doom and gloom in the Phillies' nineteenth century days. Philadelphia improved to two games over .500 in their third season in 1885, and went 71-43 the season after—for a .623 win percentage that stood as a team record until the 2011 club won 63% of their games.

1983—"Fo', fo', fo'!," was 76ers' center, Moses Malone's simplified prediction for the outcome of the 1983 NBA playoffs (foretelling a four-game sweep in each round of the postseason). To be historically accurate, it went down as "Fo', fi', fo'," but really, who's counting?

On this day in 1983, the Sixers, with a win over the Milwaukee Bucks 104-96, completed their last of seven straight playoff victories to open the postseason, a record at the time.

Philly's only loss came against Milwaukee in Game 4 of the conference championship, pushing the series to five games.

1987—Eventually, the Flyers ran into a buzz saw in the Edmonton Oilers in the Stanley Cup Finals. That is what happens when faced off against fate and a player simply referred to as, "The Great One."

But before the Flyers fell to Edmonton and the great Wayne Gretzky in Game 7 of one of the greatest Stanley Cup Finals in history (see May 31st), there was jubilation in Philadelphia, as the Fly Guys won the Wales Conference Championship on this date, 4-3 over the Montreal Canadiens in Game 6.

With the win, the Flyers were headed back to the Stanley Cup Finals for the sixth time in 14 years.

2010—With a 4-3 win over the Boston Bruins (after trailing 3-0) in the second round of the Stanley Cup playoffs, the Flyers had accomplished something few teams in pro sports have been able to even approach. They had come from three games down to win a seven-game series.

It was only the third such occurrence of such a feat in NHL history. In Major League Baseball, it's happened just once. The NBA? Never.

Benefitting from the ultimate momentum swing, the Flyers rode the wave all the way to the Cup finals, falling to the Chicago Blackhawks in six games (see June 9th).

2013—The 76ers hired Sam Hinkie away from the Houston Rockets to fill the role of President and General Manager. At the time, his analytics background shed light on his affinity for taking unique and bold perspectives on building competitive rosters; eventually, he'd be the poster boy for tanking.

Hinkie's hiring came one season after the disastrous acquisition of center Andrew Bynum following his tenure with the Lakers, and his strategy, from the outset, seemed to be to tear it all down and build through the draft. Rumors in 2015 surfaced that his initial plan may have called for a seven-year rebuilding process.

By the 2013-14 season, not a single player remained from their roster just two seasons prior. Philadelphia fans are still waiting patiently (or maybe apathetically?) for signs of life from its once-proud basketball team.

15th

1984—Arguably the Flyers' greatest player in team history, Bobby Clarke retired from the NHL after a 15-year career spent entirely with Philadelphia. He could have probably still played, but he couldn't pass up the Flyers' job offer.

Clarke is one of the few professional athletes to transition directly from player to general manager. His initial stint as GM included two trips to the Stanley Cup Finals (1985, 1987) before being terminated in 1990. He'd get another Finals trip under his belt (1997) in his second stint as GM for the Fly Guys, but never won the big one as part of the front office.

2001—The 76ers' Allen Iverson won the Maurice Podoloff Trophy as the NBA's Most Valuable Player.

Measured at six feet tall (in high-heels) and weighing just 165, AI became both the shortest and lightest league MVP.

COLOR COMMENTARY

It seems like a century ago that the Sixers ruled in the Philadelphia pro sports hierarchy and Iverson was king. It feels so long ago because they've done so little as a team since.

And it's hard to remember because the team's window of success at the time was slammed shut as quickly as it was furiously thrust open in the spring of 2001.

Coached by a legend in Larry Brown, Iverson was surrounded by a team-first supporting cast. None of Al's merry men were all-around NBA stars, but they all thrived within their roles and played suffocating defense. But let's not discount the contributions of the league MVP.

Because Al, ultimately, never won a championship, and was so tough to coach and surround with complimentary players, we may forget how great a player he actually was. The oft-frustrating star was legitimately most valuable in '01 because, truly, the team was NOTHING without Iverson. They didn't need Eric Snow, or George Lynch, or Dikembe Mutombo like they needed Iverson.

Once upon a time, Allen Iverson was the best player on one of the best teams in the NBA. It was brief, but real.

16th

1974—When one thinks of sports in Philadelphia, professional lacrosse rarely comes to mind. But lacrosse actually has deep Philly roots.

A charter member of the National Lacrosse League, the Philadelphia Wings played the first American professional lacrosse game on this date, against the Maryland Arrows, losing 14-17. They also made it to the finals during the inaugural year and lost to the Rochester Griffins, four games to two. By no fault of the Wings, one of three teams to not file for bankruptcy, the league folded in 1976 before being resurrected a decade later with the Wings leading the charge.

The only team that survived the 1974–76 experiment, the Wings are the most decorated NLL team to date, with six combined championships.

In a poll taken by the league in 2008, 62% of the NLL players concluded that the Philadelphia Wings fans screamed the "filthiest, nastiest" venom at opposing players.

Of the 11 other teams, Colorado was next at just 14%.

1980—The 76ers would have to wait for their second NBA title. On this date, rookie point guard Magic Johnson, filling in for injured center Kareem Abdul-Jabbar (can you imagine Mo Cheeks guarding the paint?), scored 42 points in the LA Lakers' Game 6 NBA Finals win (123-107) over the 76ers.

With Magic (the first rookie to win the Finals MVP) on board, the Lakers were on the verge of a dynasty. The Sixers, in need of a spark plug of their own to get over the top, would be three years and a Moses Malone away from getting that second title.

2001—On the road to the 76ers' NBA Finals appearance in '01, the team's Eastern Conference Semifinals series with the Toronto Raptors was unquestionably the most entertaining.

Already having scored 54 points in Game 2, answered by the Raptors' Vince Carter dropping 50 in Game 3, Allen Iverson scored 52 points on this date (8-for-14 from three-point territory) to become just the second player in NBA history (the other, Michael Jordan) to score 50 twice in one playoff series.

17th

1941—Happy Connie Mack Day. On this day in '41 at Shibe Park in Philadelphia, the state of Pennsylvania declared the new legal holiday to honor the longtime Philadelphia Athletics owner/manager.

To cap the celebration, Shibe Park was supposed to be re-named Connie Mack Stadium, but Mack refused the honor out of respect for Benjamin Shibe, Mack's original partner with the A's.

Shibe Park/Connie Mack Stadium, ca. 1938 (*Library of Congress*)

Inevitably, Shibe Park became Connie Mack on February 13th, 1953, three years after "The Grand Old Man of Baseball" retired from coaching.

18th

1883—The Philadelphia Dolly Vardens no. 1 and no. 2 clubs scrimmaged, amidst a modest audience in Chester, including an interested member of the *Philadelphia Times*.

Organized in 1867, the first female baseball club (and, in turn, first all-black female baseball club), the Dolly Vardens (named after a fashionable style of dress of the period), sprung up from Philadelphia and surrounding suburbs. By 1883, the club had a no. 1 and no. 2 team, which often

COLOR COMMENTARY

Unfortunately, history turns a nearly-blind eye to the Vardens, an all-black squad, which is credited as the first female baseball club. They get a blurb on a timeline of equal-rights accomplishments, but little else.

There's a lot of firsts mentioned in this book, but the Dolly Vardens baseball nine, while mostly forgotten, were true trailblazers in the sports civil rights movement. And really, both American sports and civil rights were in their infancy at this time. It's just hard to make a resounding statement when you're laying the foundation.

scrimmaged. When a *Philadelphia Times* reporter caught this particular scrimmage in 1883, the story had legs, and the Vardens had their first national recognition, as part of a story in the back pages of the *New York Times* the following day.

1912—Eight lucky Philadelphians were picked to take the field, as Detroit Tigers, for one single game against the reigning champion Philadelphia Athletics.

The Tigers' regulars refused to play, in protest of teammate Ty Cobb's indefinite suspension from Major League Baseball (he had stormed the stands days earlier and beat a fan nearly to death).

Facing a heavy fine if it had failed to field a team, Detroit, with the help of A's skipper Connie Mack, selected eight local "athletes" to dress in their stead—not to play, but simply to take the field and avoid penalty. And then Mack took advantage of a good situation.

Mack reneged on his deal to allow the Tigers to simply forfeit, and made Detroit play the game. Local gangster/boxer Billy Maharg (see October 5) played third base, and St. Joe's junior Allan Travers pitched, allowing 26 hits and every run of the A's 24-2 rout of the replacement Tigers.

Father Travers—the only priest to have ever pitched in the big leagues—still holds the record for most runs surrendered in a single 9-inning game. What a mess.

2008—Sidney Crosby and the Pittsburgh Penguins, administering a 6-0 beating in Game 5, took the Conference Championship title over the Philadelphia Flyers.

The Detroit Red Wings would take home the Stanley Cup in six games.

19th

1974—It wasn't exactly a long and arduous journey, as the Flyers, by way of a 1-0 Game 6 victory over the Boston Bruins in the Final, won the Stanley Cup for the first time in team history—in just their seventh season since entering the NHL in the '67 expansion.

They were the first expansion team to win a title, but speed wasn't necessarily their game. Those early '70s seasons marked the first of the Flyers squads affectionately known as the "Broad Street Bullies."

So legendary was the Flyers' brawler style, opposing players were thought to have contracted "Philly Flu" immediately upon stepping foot in the Spectrum. Opposing players dreaded the beating they'd inevitably take, and it wasn't just a North American bug—the Flyers' 1976 victory over the Red Army squad (see January 11th) has largely been attributed to the weak-at-the-knees Soviets falling victim to the hype before setting foot on Philly ice.

Clarke, left, and Parent, right, hoisting Lord Stanley's Cup. (*Philadelphia Flyers*)

In record time? Seven seasons of existence, and Philadelphia was officially a hockey town. Bobby Clarke, the youthful exuberant uber-captain Dave Schultz, a "goonie" if ever there was one, and Smythe Award–winning goaltender Bernie Parent (2.02 goals against average in the '74 playoffs) made it easy to be a Flyers fan. The trophy just legitimized it all.

They'd repeat in 1975 and lose in the Final in 1976. By 1980, all four of the city's pro teams, including the Flyers, were alive in their championship series, with the Phillies the lone victor. In all, it was a great time to be a Philadelphia sports fan—and it all started with this jubilant call from Philly broadcasting great Gene Hart, forever etched in Flyers lore:

"Ladies and gentlemen, the Flyers are going to win the Stanley Cup! The Flyers win the Stanley Cup! The Flyers win the Stanley Cup! The Flyers have *won* the Stanley Cup!"

20th

1951—Phillies leadoff hitter Richie Ashburn collected eight hits in a single day.

It took two games, though, in the Phils' double header sweep of the Pirates in which Philly outscored Pittsburgh, 29-4 (17-0 and 12-4 respectively). Whitey finished just one base hit shy of the Major League doubleheader hits record.

21st

1996—Phils pitcher Terry Mulholland, entering the game with the third-lowest batting average in Major League history (400 at-bats minimum), hit a 407-foot home run in the second inning—just one of 69 hits in his 20-year career. Amazingly, it was the shorter of his two career home runs, with the first coming a season prior, measuring an astonishing 437 feet.

After the game, Mulholland mused, "Most great power hitters don't hit for a high average."

22nd

1963—In 1962, Philadelphia had lost its NBA team (Warriors) and hometown hero (Wilt Chamberlain). By 1964, both would be back in the City of Brotherly Love, with championship aspirations looming.

On this date in 1963, the NBA approved the move of the Syracuse Nationals to the city of Philadelphia. Philly businessmen Irv Kosloff and Ike Richman purchased the team with intentions to restore professional basketball to the city one year after the Warriors had split for San Francisco.

By the team's fourth season in the city, both Wilt Chamberlain and the NBA championship trophy were back in Philadelphia.

23rd

1887—The National Colored League, the first (though brief) all-black baseball league, folded on this date, with the Philadelphia Pythians as its all-time winningest club, at just 4-1.

The Pythians, organized by the fraternal organization The Knights of Pythias, was Philadelphia's first African American baseball club. Once the team folded on May 18th, the league, founded in Pennsylvania and counting on Philly as one of its strongholds in the region, regrettably abandoned the notion. Essentially, the league was helplessly ahead of its time.

It would be over 20 years until Negro League baseball would return to Philadelphia, as the Hilldale FC and Philadelphia Giants would provide the success and staying power necessary to help bring about change in American professional baseball in the twenty-first century.

24th

1980—Down 3-2 in the Stanley Cup Finals series, the Flyers took the New York Islanders to overtime in Game 6. Isles winger Bob Nystrom scored the game-winner (the Islanders won 5-4), spoiling what would have been a Game 7 homecoming for the surging Flyers. Linesman Leon Stickle admitted after the game that he should have whistled New York offside on a scoring play in regulation that gave the Isles a 2-1 lead.

With the win, the Islanders secured their first Stanley Cup.

COLOR COMMENTARY

This was the most poorly officiated game in the history of the NHL. The Islanders were awarded, by all counts, two goals that should not have counted, due to an apparent Denis Potvin high stick, and the blown offsides call by Stickle. As for the game winner in OT, Nystrom may have indeed held the line there for the Cup, but I'm still too agitated to think rationally.

I remember this being a weekend afternoon game in May, and wanting it so badly to go to a decisive seventh game. Despite the Flyers' third period rally to tie the game at 4-4, it just wasn't meant to be. This devastating loss capped off a great season of Flyers hockey in which we saw the team go on a 35-game unbeaten streak.

It also continued the Flyers' luck of meeting teams in the finals who had been or were about to be multiple-Cup winners. They lost in '76 to Montreal, starting the Habs' run of four in a row, and this defeat to the Islanders sparked New York to three more consecutive cups. The Flyers would also lose twice more in the finals during the '80s, both times to Wayne Gretzky and the Edmonton Oilers dynasty.

25th

1997—With a 4-2 win over the New York Rangers in the Eastern Conference championship, the Flyers advanced to their seventh Stanley Cup Finals in team history.

Winger Rod Brind'Amour scored both the go-ahead and final goals of the game, giving the team a clinching 4-1 series edge.

The Cup Finals, however, was a different story. Outscoring the Flyers 16-6, the Detroit Red Wings attacked goaltenders Ron Hextall and Garth Snow, while neutralizing the suddenly fading star Eric Lindros. It was a four-game sweep for Detroit. The Flyers would wait 13 years for a return trip to the Finals in 2010.

26th

2003—Larry Brown resigned as coach of the 76ers. A week later, he signed with the Detroit Pistons.

Coaching his seventh NBA team, Brown won the title with Detroit in '04, his first and only championship in the league. But his well-traveled ways were not over.

Brown, after stops with the New York Knicks (2005–06) and Charlotte Bobcats (2008–10), is one NBA head coaching job away from double digits.

He is currently the head coach of the SMU Mustangs Men's Basketball team.

27th

In addition to the Conn Smythe, Parent earned Vezina Trophy honors as the league's top goaltender in 1975 and 1976.
(Philadephia Flyers)

1975—The Flyers wasted little time winning their second Stanley Cup in franchise history, repeating for the title in just their ninth year in existence. They defeated the Buffalo Sabres in Game 6 on this date, 2-0.

Allowing just 12 goals in the series, capped by a shutout for the second straight season, goalie Bernie Parent won his second consecutive Conn Smythe Trophy (this time with a 1.89 goals against average), awarded to the MVP of the playoffs. To this day, Mario Lemieux is the only other player to have won it twice.

It was the last team comprised completely of Canadian-born players to win the Cup.

28th

1930—Grover Cleveland Alexander, pitching in relief for the Phillies in a 5-1 loss to the Boston Braves, finished his 20-season career where it started.

"Ol' Pete" led the league in wins five times in his first seven seasons in Philadelphia (including his 1911 rookie season), and *averaged* 30 wins (and 35 complete games) in a four-year stretch from 1914 to 1917. While his performance shifted toward mediocrity in the second half of his career, spent mostly with the Chicago Cubs, Alexander pitched as well in the '10s as any other pitcher in any other decade.

Reacquired via trade in the offseason, the 43-year-old Hall of Famer was at the end of his rope in 1930, and hung them up on this day, finishing tied with Christy Mathewson for third on the all-time Major League wins list, with 373.

Bain News Service

29th

1989—Mike Schmidt, in a tearful press conference in San Diego, announced his retirement from baseball.

"Some 18 years ago I left Dayton, Ohio, with two very bad knees . . . and a dream to become a Major League Baseball player," sobbed Schmidt, "I thank God that dream came true."

After 18 years with the franchise, the Phillies' greatest player—and at times the fan base's most troubling conundrum—had, for maybe the first time, opened up his heart to Philadelphia.

2010—The Phillies knew they had a great pitcher in Roy Halladay when they signed him to a free agent deal in the offseason, but on this day, Doc was perfect.

Halladay sat down all 27 Marlins batters at Miami's Sun Life Stadium, recording the 20th perfect game in Major League Baseball history, the second in club history (see June 21st) and, incredibly, the second of the 2010 season. The 20-day differential between Dallas Braden's perfecto for Oakland on May 9th, and Halladay's, is the shortest since the first two such games were hurled in the 1880's.

Another fun fact: It's the sixth perfect game in which no earned runs were scored. The Phils notched the 1-0 lead by way of a three-base error by center fielder Cameron Maybin that allowed Chase Utley to knock in Wilson Valdez for the difference maker. What would've happened had the game been locked at 0 going into extra innings? Halladay would have to keep his heroics up until whichever inning the game ended on to get credited with the feat. A nine-inning perfecto that gets scrapped in extras is nothing more than a solid outing by rule book standards.

Meanwhile, in Chicago...

The Chicago Blackhawks hosted the Flyers in the first game of the Stanley Cup Finals, but the Fly Guys were far from perfect. In an exciting back-and-forth that featured six separate tie scores and four lead changes, the Flyers came out on the losing end, 6-5, at Chicago's United Center.

Philadelphia would ultimately lose the hard-fought series after an overtime goal in Game 6 by team MVP Patrick Kane sealed it for Chicago.

COLOR COMMENTARY

What a night to be a talk radio host. I was doing the evening shift for WIP. Of course, it was Game 1 of the Stanley Cup Finals, so my interest was fully on the hockey game. However, I did have the Phillies on one of the televisions in the studio. After all, it was just another regular season game for the Fightin's against the lowly Marlins, but I knew our audience would want to talk Phillies as well.

It was a fantastic first period. The Flyers came out fast. They led 3-2 after one period. I remember thinking, if this team could get just average goaltending, they'd win their first Cup since 1975. I'll stop there, because my blood is beginning to boil. You all know the rest; the Flyers lost

Game 1 6-5, and the series in six games, mostly due to the poor play of goaltender Michael Leighton.

It was late in the third period, when I realized Halladay had something great going, something perfect! I kept switching my attention back and forth, and when the game got to the ninth inning, I was on the edge of my seat. Halladay's gem took the sting off the Flyers' loss, but it was a rather bittersweet night on the air.

30th

1935—Phillies pitcher Jim Bivin forced a groundout to Boston Braves outfielder Babe Ruth, in the Yankee great's final at-bat in the Major Leagues.

Philadelphia won the game at Baker Bowl, 11-6.

Ruth, arguably the game's greatest, most storied legend, hit just .181 in 72 at-bats that season. Six of his 13 hits were homers.

With 714 home runs, Ruth is currently third on the all-time list, behind Hank Aaron (755) and Barry Bonds (762). But his career 1.164 OPS (on base percentage + slugging percentage) is still tops in Major League history.

31st

1983—The 76ers' 1982–83 championship season came to its victorious finale, with a 115-108 win and as part of a sweep of the LA Lakers. The celebration began on May 31st, but in actuality, spanned the entire season.

No team in any professional sport can claim victory on day one, but the Sixers certainly began with a potent recipe for success. Future Hall of Famers Julius Erving and Moses Malone led the squad, with an All-Star supporting cast including Andrew Toney, Mo Cheeks, and Bobby Jones, all potent in their own right. They dominated the regular season, going 65-17—far and away the best record in basketball—and the playoffs were no different.

The Sixers lost just one game in the postseason, going 12-1 overall, a record at the time. They swept the LA Lakers, winning what would turn out to be the last professional championship Philadelphia would claim for 25 years.

COLOR COMMENTARY

What gets lost in all this is the legacy that was defined on that day. If not for the championship, Julius "Dr. J" Erving's career might be seen much differently.

Coming over from the ABA's Nets in 1976, Dr. J immediately became the NBA's marquee player, filling both seats and stat sheets at an alarming rate. He had two ABA championships in his pocket and a Finals appearance in his first Sixers season (albeit a losing effort to Bill Walton's Portland Trail Blazers).

But just getting to the big game means little in the end (just ask Donovan McNabb). The championship in 1983 gave Philadelphia a champion, and made a winner out of its most exciting player.

1987—Oh, so close. In a rematch of the '85 Finals, the Flyers nearly topped the game's greatest player, Wayne Gretzky, and perhaps greatest team, the Edmonton Oilers, in a crushing Game 7 disappointment.

Despite an early 1-0 lead, the Flyers couldn't match the Oilers' tempo. Edmonton tied it up midway through the first period, and took the lead in the second on what would prove to be the game-winning goal by Jari Kurri. The Oilers added an insurance goal in the third to take the game (3-1), and their third Cup title in four years.

COLOR COMMENTARY

So May 31st was good to us Philadelphians in 1983, but it struck a different chord four years later.

I can remember in later years discussing this series with Flyers' legendary announcer Gene Hart and recalling his description of this series as the greatest finals he'd ever seen. And I agree, still to this day, that it was just an awesome seven games of hockey.

In the end, the Flyers were just too banged up and running on empty to defeat the mighty Oilers' dynasty. However, this was a thrilling series, with the outcome remaining in doubt right up until Glenn Anderson's late third period goal, which gave Edmonton the 3-1 lead.

When the puck squirted through goaltender Ron Hextall's pads, Hextall immediately dropped his head, knowing that was going to be it for his team. We all knew it as well.

What a fantastic series, and in terms of heartbreakers, it can be listed amongst the top three of all time in Philadelphia.

1st

1988—Paul Holmgren, a right winger for nine seasons with the Flyers (1975–84), became the team's first former player to be named head coach. While Holmgren compiled just a .459 win percentage over four seasons behind the bench, he's worked his way up the ladder, serving as the team's Assistant General Manager starting in 1998–99, and succeeding Bob Clarke as General Manager in 2006–2007.

2nd

1997—The Phillies selected J. D. Drew, from Florida State University, with the no. 2 overall pick in the Major League Baseball amateur draft. However, Drew elected not to sign with the Phils—a move that furthered the vilification of Drew's agent, Scott Boras, and sports agents in general.

Despite his no. 2 selection in the draft, J. D. was, and perhaps still is, Public Sports Enemy No. 1 in the City of Brotherly Love.

COLOR COMMENTARY

Twenty spots later (22nd overall), Jayson Werth was selected by the Baltimore Orioles. Werth, due mostly to injuries, flamed out after stints in Baltimore and LA, before winning a World Series with the Phillies in 2008, and garnering an All-Star selection in 2009. In the end, things have a way of working out. But Drew is still dead to me.

2002—Phillies pitcher Robert Person hit two home runs, including a grand slam, while tossing five shutout innings in an 18-3 pummeling of the Expos at Veterans Stadium.

Person's seven RBI are still a modern era record for Phils pitchers, besting the five-RBI outings of Rick Wise in 1971 and Jack Knight in 1926.

2008—With a home run in the first inning of a 5-4 win over the Cincinnati Reds at Citizens Bank Park, Chase Utley became the first Phillie with two separate five-game home run streaks—and he did it in the same season.

Utley's first stretch of five games with at least one homer was from April 17-21. The five-game mark (either one) is a Phillies record, shared with Bobby Abreu, Mike Schmidt, and Dick Allen. Utley hit exactly 1/3 of his total home runs of 2008 in those ten games (11 of 33).

3rd

1975—On this date, the Flyers made a couple influential moves in the 1975 NHL entry draft for ultimately insignificant hockey players.

Trading the 18th pick, Don McLean, and current team broadcaster Bill Clement, the Flyers wrestled the no. 1 overall pick away from the Washington Capitals. While their selection, Mel Bridgman, was a serviceable center in 17 pro seasons, he never quite lived up to expectations.

In addition, the Flyers made history with the final pick in the ninth round, drafting the league's first Soviet-born player in Viktor Khatulev. The pick was a throw-away, however, as the USSR had no intentions of releasing the young left winger to the NHL. Khatulev himself hadn't heard of his draft selection until 1978.

4th

1964—One of the greatest pitching performances by one of the great power pitchers in baseball history came against the Philadelphia Phillies on this date.

Sandy Koufax, of the Los Angeles Dodgers, faced the minimum 27 batters in a 91-pitch, no-hit performance with just a single walk (to Richie Allen, later out on a double play), ruining the perfect game bid.

The Phils' Jim Bunning one-upped Koufax 17 days later against the Mets, tossing a "27 up, 27 down" perfect game (see June 21st).

5th

1977—Dr. J and the Sixers were at the start of something big. Their efforts wouldn't bear fruit until the '83 championship season, but in '77 they had as good a shot as ever. Holding a 2-0 Finals lead over the Portland Trail Blazers, the Sixers were in position to win their second title, and first in a decade. And then the wheels came off.

On June 5th, 1977, the 76ers lost their fourth straight game, and the NBA title, to the Blazers, the first team in NBA history to win a Finals in such fashion.

Julius Erving, in his first year with Philadelphia, would need a few more seasons to win the title. But proof of his stardom carrying over from the defunct ABA was alive and well.

2004—It's a thrilling moment, and familiar call from exulted track announcers, when a race horse "wins by a nose." On

The Labor Day Pennsylvania Derby at Parx Casino was renamed in Smarty Jones' honor in 2010. (*Just chaos*)

this occasion, however, the big story was about the *second* nose to cross the finish line, that of Smarty Jones, a two-year-old thoroughbred from Chester County's Someday Farm. Finishing a mere schnoz-and-a-half behind long shot Birdstone in the Belmont Stakes, Smarty Jones, ridden by jockey Stewart Elliott, fell one victory shy (after winning the Kentucky Derby and Preakness) of becoming the first horse since Affirmed in 1978 to achieve horse racing's elusive Triple Crown.

6th

2001—For only the second time in NBA playoffs history, two opposing players put up over 40 points in the same game, as Allen Iverson's 48 helped the 76ers take Game 1 of the NBA Finals from Shaquille O'Neal (44 points) and the LA Lakers, 107-101, in overtime.

Iverson, never a prototypical team player, cut loose in the 2000–01 season, earning MVP honors, while leading the Sixers to an East-best 56-26 record—but he didn't do it alone. For perhaps the only time in his career, AI had the right group of talent surrounding him, including Defensive Player of the Year Dikembe Mutombo (acquired in a midseason trade for Theo Ratliff), top Sixth Man Aaron McKie, and defensive stalwarts Eric Snow and George Lynch.

It took an extra period to do the job, but as AI drained a late three in OT, poignantly stepping over fallen Laker Tyronn Lue, the Sixers had the permanent lead.

They had a win (107-101), and a chance—two things most experts hadn't expected, especially in the wake of the Lakers' undefeated playoff run to that point.

COLOR COMMENTARY

I have never considered myself a big fan of the NBA. Nevertheless, I am a Philadelphian, and I root for our success. Throughout the countless fantastic seasons of the Eagles, Phillies, and Flyers that I had enjoyed over the years, I can honestly say that this season of Sixers basketball simply thrilled me.

Who can forget the *Daily News* and all their covers depicting the Sixers or all the cars driving around town with the Sixers flags on them? What a fantastic season of basketball, and an incredible postseason run.

I can remember thinking if the Sixers could just get one in LA, they would have a chance for the title. Well, they got Game 1, and AI gave us a lasting memory stepping over Lue, but sadly, they lost the next four.

It can be said that people will indeed remember the Lakers winning that series, but no one will ever forget AI and the closing minutes of Game 1!

7th

1987—In front of over 43,000 fans at the Vet, Phillies rookie starter Mike Jackson tossed eight innings of no-hit ball against the Montreal Expos, before losing his no-no bid to a Tim Raines leadoff double in the ninth.

It was the final season in Philly for Jackson, who is most recognized for being a talented relief pitcher for other teams. Saving 40 games for the Indians in 1998, he posted a 1.55 ERA. He returned to Philadelphia in 2000, but an arm injury cost him the season before he ever threw a pitch.

1997—On this date in '97, the high point of the Lindros Era would take a swift turn, as the Flyers were bounced in four games by the Detroit Red Wings in the Stanley Cup Finals. Lindros' only goal of the series came in the final minute of the final game. It was a successful season, but five years into the Lindros Era, immediate Stanley Cup expectations had gone from inevitable to questionable—no. 88, perhaps for the first time, was on notice.

8th

1989—"It ain't over 'til it's over"—Yogi Berra

On this date in 1989, the Pittsburgh Pirates put 10 runs on the board in the first inning at Vet Stadium, prompting the Buccos' broadcaster, Jim Rooker, to proclaim, "If we lose this game, I'll walk home."

The Phillies immediately whittled away, with two runs in the bottom of the first, and the comeback was on.

Trailing just 11-10 in the bottom of the eighth inning, the Phils tacked on five more runs to take the lead and, eventually, the game, 15-11.

In the offseason, Rooker made good on his promise, raising nearly $100k in a 13-day charity walk from Philadelphia to Pittsburgh.

9th

2010—The Flyers lost Game 6 of the Stanley Cup Finals (4-3 in OT), and the series, to the Chicago Blackhawks. It was the Flyers' first Finals appearance since 1997.

The Fly Guys, coached by midseason hire Peter Laviolette, won a shootout in the last game of the season to make the playoffs, overcame a virtually impossible 0-3 hole in the second round, and wrestled attention away from the headline-hogging Phillies. But, of course, they failed to bring home the Cup.

10th

1972—In a 15-3 blowout of the Phillies, Hank Aaron moved past Willie Mays into second place on the career home run list, with his 649th shot. Aaron (755 career home runs), who would supplant Babe Ruth (714) for the top spot in 1974, made a habit of earning career benchmarks at the expense of the Phils—his 700th home run (1974) also came against the Fightin's.

11th

1910—The Hilldale Field Club of Darby, PA, one of the Philadelphia area's most successful African American baseball clubs, played its first game, a 5-10 loss to Lansdowne.

The Monarchs, left, and Hilldale Club, right, lining up before the 1924
Series (*Photo by J.E. Mille[r], K.C.*)

Originally a fourteen/fifteen-year-old league, the Hilldale
FC developed into a powerhouse of men's professional negro
league baseball, capturing the first two Eastern Colored League
crowns, and meeting the Kansas City Monarchs (of the Negro
National League) in 1924 for the first-ever Negro League
World Series (a four games to five Hilldale loss). Hilldale and
Kansas City met again in the series the following year. This
time Hilldale was victorious, five games to one.

12th

1959—Philadelphia great Richie Ashburn singled in a game
in which the Phillies were no-hit by San Francisco Giants
hurler Mike McCormick.

Confused?

Ashburn's hit in the sixth inning was nullified by a rain-
out, and the game was final through just five frames (3-0,
Giants).

In 1991, a rule change required all official no-hitters be
completed in at least nine innings of play. McCormick's no-no
was one of 36 to be wiped off the record books.

13th

1995—The Flyers lost Game 6 of the Conference Finals, 4-2, and the New Jersey Devils were headed to their first-ever Stanley Cup Finals.

The Devils, led by the young phenom goalie Martin Brodeur, would eventually win the Cup, securing the state of New Jersey's first major sports championship.

Brodeur, currently the NHL's all-time leader in regular season wins, was enjoying his first full season as the Devils' primarily goaltender in 1994–95. He would lead the Devils to three Stanley Cup Finals in all, while Eric Lindros, the Flyers' own young superstar at the time, never quite delivered.

14th

2005—Seattle Mariners outfielder Ichiro Suzuki became the third player since 1900 to collect 1,000 base hits in under 700 games (696), in a 3-1 defeat of the Philadelphia Phillies.

Before Ichiro, Phillies great Chuck Klein was the last person to do it, getting his 1,000th hit in his 683rd game in 1933.

15th

1909—Bala Cynwyd native Ben Shibe, part owner of the Athletics (1901–22) and namesake of Shibe Park in Philadelphia, received a US patent on this date for his cork-center baseball. Spalding was the first company to manufacture the ball, which remains (with a few alterations) in the game today.

The cork/rubber core baseball, left, was replaced in 1943 due to a wartime rubber shortage. To the right, the controversially "dead" predominantly cork core ball (*Roger Smith*).

1991—Phillies right-hander Andy Ashby became the first player in franchise history to strike out three batters in an inning using the minimum nine pitches. Oddly (though not atypical for him in a Phils uniform), Ashby lasted just five innings in the 3-1 loss to the Cincinnati Reds, totaling five strikeouts. In 2011, reliever Juan Perez became the only other Phillie to accomplish the feat.

Side note: For the Philadelphia Athletics, Hall of Famers Rube Waddell (1902) and Lefty Grove (twice, 1928) both pulled off the tricky feat.

2001—Allen Iverson and his band of also-rans ultimately were no match for the all-time duo of Shaquille O'Neal and Kobe Bryant of the LA Lakers.

Despite a thrilling Game 1 victory in Los Angeles, the Sixers could do no more, dropping the NBA Finals to the Lakers on this night, in Game 5, 108-96.

It was the Sixers' sixth trip to the Finals, and fourth straight against the Lakers.

16th

1986—Proving the franchise hadn't learned its lesson the first time with its trade of Wilt Chamberlain in 1968, the 76ers dealt Moses Malone, a center with plenty of prime years remaining, to the Washington Bullets (along with first-round draft picks in 1986 and 1988). The Sixers got Jeff Ruland and Cliff Robinson in return, neither of whom played more than three seasons with the team.

With Malone gone and Julius Erving about to enter his final season in pro basketball, the Sixers were effectively finished. While Charles Barkley and Allen Iverson both had marginal success in the aftermath, it could be said that the team is still searching for its next Malone.

17th

1876—Participants in the first season of play for Major League Baseball, naturally, set a lot of records. By season's end, George Hall, of the Philadelphia Athletics, had the first single-season home run mark—with just five.

On this date in MLB's inaugural season, Hall was also the first player to hit two home runs in a single game.

COLOR COMMENTARY

Home run records and controversy are a natural connection, as old as the game itself—whether it be Roger Maris' toppling of Babe Ruth's record in '61, by way of a modern elongated 162-game season, or the steroid stench attached to each memorable blast from the likes of Barry Bonds, Mark McGwire, Sammy Sosa, etc. But even the first-ever home run champion was not free of scandal—in 1877, George Hall and three others were banned for life after conspiring to throw games for the Louisville Grays. It doesn't delegitimize his record, but it shows that mischievous characters and practices are nothing new for America's pasttime.

18th

1948—Phils' pitching great Robin Roberts made his Major League debut on this date, losing to the Pittsburgh Pirates 2-0.

The Hall of Famer pitched 14 seasons in Philadelphia, finishing second to Steve Carlton in career wins for the organization (234), while currently sitting 27th on the league's all-time list (286).

The Phillies retired Roberts' no. 36 uniform in 1962, and in 1999 the franchise's best right-hander ranked 74th on the *Sporting News*' 100 Greatest Baseball Players list.

1950—In a 21-2 drubbing of the Philadelphia Athletics, the Cleveland Indians scored 14 runs in the first inning of play—an opening frame AL record that still stands (the Boston Red Sox matched the mark against the Florida Marlins during interleague play in 2003).

19th

1955—In a 1-0 victory over the Chicago Cubs, the Phillies tied a record for the longest shutout in club history. Winning pitcher Jack Meyer tossed more innings in relief (eight) than Phils starter Ron Negray (seven).

1984—With the no. 5 overall pick in the 1984 draft, the 76ers selected Charles Barkley, a forward from Auburn.

An easy pick at the time, with the no. 5 slot in the draft, the Sixers' all-time leading rebounder was essentially traded for when he was just 16 years old.

Six years earlier in 1978, Philadelphia attained the draft pick in a deal that sent young guard World B. Free to the San Diego Clippers. And although Free would go on to average 20.3 points per game in his 13-year career, the Sixers would have a championship in hand (1983) and a future Hall of Fame forward in Barkley waiting in the wings.

20th

1967—Phillies pitcher Larry Jackson pitched a one-hitter in a 4-0 win, personally besting the New York Mets for the 18th straight time. A very cool fact, and one that made Larry probably very proud. However, the name Larry Jackson likely invokes a different memory for Philadelphia sports fans; he was involved in one of the worst trades in Phillies history.

In early 1966, Jackson was acquired by the Phillies along with another starter, Bob Buhl, from the Chicago Cubs. In the deal, the Phillies gave up utility player John Herrnstein, outfield prospect Adolfo Phillips, and a little-known right-handed reliever named Ferguson Jenkins.

Of course, Jenkins developed into a dominant starter, compiling a 284-226 record, 3.34 ERA, and 3,192 career strikeouts. A three-time All-Star and Cy Young Award winner in 1971, Jenkins became the first Canadian to be inducted into the Baseball Hall of Fame.

21st

1907—Scottish golfer Alec Ross won the 13th US Open golf tournament, held for the first time locally, at the Philadelphia Cricket Club's St. Martin's course.

The Philadelphia Cricket Club is one of the oldest country clubs in the nation, having served as the original host of the US Women's National Singles Championship (tennis), and twice hosting golf's US Open (Ross' countryman, Alex Smith of Scotland, won in 1910).

1964—Happy Father's Day to Jim Bunning. On this date, Bunning, father of nine, pitched a perfect game for the Phillies, shutting down all 27 Mets batters in a 6-0 win at Shea Stadium. It was the first of the century for the National League, and stood as the Phils' lone perfecto until Roy Halladay duplicated the feat in 2010.

Bunning's perfecto came in the first game of a doubleheader. Rick Wise pitched the second game, surrendering just three hits to the Mets.

The final tally? One day, two games, 18 innings, zero earned runs, and just three singles for New York. Pretty amazin'.

Philadelphia Cricket Club's insignia outside its Flourtown location, featuring two 18-hole golf courses (*Michael Kirk*)

22nd

1991—With the sixth overall pick in the 1991 NHL entry draft, the Flyers selected center Peter Forsberg. Forsberg didn't stay long for Philadelphia, as he was moved a year later to the Quebec Nordiques as the key player in the deal for Eric Lindros (see June 30th). Forsberg, the 2002–03 league MVP, would return to the Orange & Black nearly 15 years later.

Quebec, which drafted Lindros on this date with the no. 1 overall pick, saw its prized selection sit out the entire season before being dealt to Philly.

23rd

1971—It was perhaps the greatest overall single-game performance by a Major League pitcher.

Phillies right-hander Rick Wise recorded the only no-hitter of his career, in a 4-0 win. And although his lone walk surrendered to the Cincinnati squad prevented the outing from being "perfect," what Wise did with the *bat* is what made the performance, arguably, the greatest.

Wise hit not one, but two home runs on a day that Pete Rose, Johnny Bench, Tony Perez, and the rest of the Reds' Big Red Machine couldn't even squeak out an infield single.

Wise became the third player in Major League history with a home run in a no-hit performance, and the first to hit a pair.

A walking Quizzo trivia answer, Wise also pitched for the Phillies the night of Jim Bunning's no-hitter (see June 21st)—he threw the second game of the doubleheader after Bunning sent all 27 batters down in the opener.

2012—In his second turn with the team, slugger Jim Thome clubbed his 609th career home run—a game-ending solo shot that lifted the Phillies to a 7-6 victory over the visiting Tampa Bay Rays at Citizens Bank Park. It was the first career pinch-hit walk-off for Thome, but by no means was it unfamiliar territory.

With the timely opposite field blast, Thome moved past Babe Ruth for the top spot on baseball's all-time walk-off home run list, with 13.

24th

1963—33-year-old boxing legend Joey Giardello of South Philly won a major upset decision over Sugar Ray Robinson

(10 rounds) to become the no. 1 challenger for the middle-weight title.

Giardello won the title a year later over Dick Tiger in Atlantic City, to begin a two-year reign at the top of the middleweight standings.

25th

1971—Willie Stargell hit what is thought to be the longest home run ever at Veterans Stadium. The amazing part? Stargell hit the tremendous blast during the Vet's inaugural season, and the record stood until the stadium's demolition over 30 years later.

In September of 1982, the Phillies recognized the Pirates' future Hall of Famer by unveiling a star in section 601 where the ball had landed.

That had to hurt. Brown (99), seconds from pouncing on Hall of Fame QB, Joe Montana. (*Philadelphia Eagles*)

1992—Coming off two consecutive All-Pro seasons, defensive tackle Jerome Brown died on this day, in both the prime of his life and career. The 6'2", 292(+)-pound behemoth was a monster up the middle, earning first team All-NFL (AP) honors his final two years of play.

Brown and nephew Gus were both killed following an accident in which Brown's corvette had skidded and flipped off the road, while traveling at a high rate of speed in his hometown of Brooksville, Florida.

Hall of Famer and Eagles legend Reggie White said of his fallen teammate, "[He was] one of the greatest men I ever knew in my life."

2010—The Toronto Blue Jays played a home game—at the Phils' Citizens Bank Park.

Citing safety concerns surrounding the G-20 Summit in Toronto, the interleague game and series was moved to Philadelphia, where the Phillies played for the first time as the "visiting" squad. It was the first regular season game in which a designated hitter was used in a National League park.

The Phils' Roy Halladay pitched seven shutout innings in the 9-0 victory over his former team.

26th

2001—The Campbell Soup Company announced a deal to sign Eagles quarterback Donovan McNabb and the St. Louis Rams' Kurt Warner to the *Chunky Soup* brand's "largest sports marketing effort in history."

In Philadelphia, *Chunky Soup* would become synonymous with the Birds' QB, for better or worse. When McNabb reportedly threw up in the huddle during Super Bowl XXXIX, speculation, in jest, regarding his pre-game meal was only natural.

27th

1963—Tony Gonzalez, a solid, if unspectacular, Phillies outfielder, ended his then-record errorless streak on this date at 205 games.

In eight-plus seasons in Philadelphia, Gonzalez committed just 25 errors, while hitting as high as .339 from the plate in 1967. The scrappy hitter had a knack for getting on base at all costs—after years among the league leaders in hit-by-pitches, Gonzalez became the first player in league history to wear a helmet with a protective ear-flap.

In addition to Gonzalez's historically rare error, Johnny Callison became one of just seven Phillies in franchise history to hit for the cycle on this date, a 13-4 Phillies win over the Pittsburgh Pirates.

28th

2001—In a ground-breaking ceremony before an evening game against the Florida Marlins, the plans for the Phillies' new ballpark were unveiled, along with the location of the left field foul pole after a postgame fireworks display. Two years later, Citizens Bank purchased the park's naming rights, in a 25-year, $95 million deal.

2004—In a 14-6 win over the Montreal Expos, Phils third baseman David Bell hit just the eighth cycle in Phillies history. David joined his grandfather Gus Bell, and the pair became the first grandfather-grandson combo to hit a single, double, triple, and home run in a single game.

Gus hit his cycle in 1951 against the Phillies, at Shibe Park.

29th

1985—In an interview published by the *Montreal Gazette* on this date, Mike Schmidt had the Philadelphia fans in his crosshairs.

Schmidt was particularly criticized for his statement about the Philly fans, "Whatever I've got in my career now, I

would have a great deal more if I'd played in Los Angeles or Chicago—you name a town—a place where the fans were just grateful to have me around."

He apologized and softened his stance in the days that followed, and even showed up for pre-game warmups on July 1st at the Vet in a long dark wig and sunglasses—a visual display of humility that was greeted with applause by the Philly faithful.

(AP Photo/Peter Morgan)

30th

1992—It was a trade that would define an era of Flyers hockey. Steve Duchesne, Peter Forsberg, Ron Hextall, Kerry Huffman, Mike Ricci, Chris Simon, two first-round picks, and $15 million (nearly enough to cover the Quebec/Colorado payroll for its '92 and '93 seasons combined) headed to the Quebec Nordiques (Colorado Avalanche), and Eric Lindros—JUST Eric Lindros—was Philadelphia bound. The first overall pick in the draft, Lindros did not disappoint early on, winning the Hart Trophy and leading the Flyers to a Stanley Cup Finals in 1997. What he'll be remembered most for, however, are the negatives—the concussions, the attitude, his meddling parents, and Peter Forsberg's ascension to greatness.

COLOR COMMENTARY

Another one of those moments when you remember where you were. I was parked in my car, listening to the live conference call on WIP, outside a restaurant for a scheduled lunch date. She was going to have to wait. The Flyers were more important. This was a big deal in Philadelphia.

After five days of depositions, 11 witnesses, 400 pages of documents, and an eight-page decision, Arbitrator Larry Bertuzzi awarded #88 to the Flyers, instead of the New York Rangers.

This was 1992, and the Flyers were in rebuild mode. This deal invigorated the fan base, and a town celebrated the "Next One."

All in all, even though Lindros was never able to win a cup here, his style of play and his great Flyers seasons made the pricey deal still worth it to me. It can be said that the Flyers lost out on Peter Forsberg, and this deal eventually helped Quebec/Colorado win a cup, but the years spent watching #88 were memorable ones indeed.

1993—The 76ers selected, with the no. 2 pick in the NBA draft, a rail-thin Mormon missionary who hadn't played organized basketball in two years. Shawn Bradley, at 7'6", the league's third-tallest player in history, enjoyed a 12-year career that never quite matched the hype.

COLOR COMMENTARY

He lacked aggressiveness, strength, and desire to succeed in the highest ranks—but he was seven feet, six inches tall . . . so nothing else seemed to matter, not even his name. He was 7'6", and wore #76 for the 76ers—a fun piece of redundancy that would serve as a painful reminder of why he was drafted, and how he secured a $44 million NBA contract. The name on the back of the jersey seemed as irrelevant as the skinny frame and timid personality that filled it.

After flaming out just two and a half seasons into his six-year contract with Philadelphia, the 7'6" illusion dissolved, as Bradley was shipped to New Jersey, donning a #45 jersey and taking his appropriate place as one of the NBA's top backup centers.

Admittedly, the awkward, bony, freakishly tall super-man with an illogically tame, boyish demeanor was at least fun to watch—though, maybe for all the wrong reasons.

1st

1901—The Phillies defeated the Pittsburgh Pirates 1-0. With the loss, the Pirates became the only team during the twentieth century to be blanked just once in a full Major League Baseball season.

The all-time National League record belongs to the 1894 Phils, who played a full 132-game season without being shut out. That year, all three Phillies outfielders (Hall of Famers Ed Delahanty, Billy Hamilton, and Sam Thompson) batted over .400.

1958—Phillies first baseman Ed Bouchee, *Sporting News* Rookie of the Year in 1957, was reinstated by Major League Baseball after receiving a sentence of three years probation for indecent exposure.

Baseball commissioner Ford C. Frick allowed Bouchee to return to the Phils after three months of treatment at a Connecticut psychiatric institution.

Frick released the following statement:

It was the only decision I could live with... I have made an exhaustive study of all the evidence and I am convinced Bouchee is completely cured... If there was any evidence that he would fail again, I would not have reinstated him. I am assuming sole and complete responsibility.

2nd

1993—The Phillies lost Game 1 of a doubleheader to the San Diego Padres, 5-2, in an eight-and-a-half-hour game delayed by nearly six hours of rain delays. Ending at 1:03 a.m., surely, they'd call off the second game, right?

After a half-hour break, the umpires decided to play on, with a Major League Baseball first—a 1:30 a.m. start time . . .
(continued on July 3rd)

3rd

1993—The second game of the Phils' doubleheader ended at 4:41 a.m. (in extra innings!), the latest conclusion in Major League history. Closer Mitch Williams knocked in the winning run (6-5), in his only at-bat of the season, in the 10th inning, bringing an end to the 12-hour marathon—sort of. The Phils still had to play their scheduled July 3rd game later that evening.

At 9:57 p.m., the Phillies had concluded their third game in a single 24-hour day, losing to the Padres, 6-4.

COLOR COMMENTARY

Believe it or not, I stayed up the entire doubleheader and watched every hour of programming for the entire 12 hours.

Oddly enough, I received a call on my bulky, 1993 cell phone at around 2 a.m. from my buddy asking me if I wanted to go down to The Vet for Game 2. He screamed, "They're letting people in for free!"

In retrospect, I should've gone. This was one for the ages, but I decided to have yet another beer and enjoy from the friendly confines of home.

Funny thing though, this was just one of the hundreds of memories from that magical 1993 season, a season that remains my favorite of all time.

4th

1934—Walter "Boom Boom" Beck earned his nickname at Hack Wilson's expense.

Upset with being pulled from a game in Philadelphia, pitcher Beck of the Brooklyn Dodgers spun around and hurled the ball toward right field—where teammate Wilson, a noted after-hours wild man, had reportedly fallen fast asleep against the wall.

The ball "boom-boomed" against the tin-plated Baker Bowl fence and into center field, startling Wilson. Dazed and confused, Wilson chased after the ball and fired it to second base, thinking the game had resumed, and the ball was in play.

It was a telling incident for the enigmatic, and alcoholic, Hall of Famer Wilson, who was dropped by the Dodgers a month later. And after a six-game stint in Philly, he was out of baseball for good.

1938—Contrary to the spirit of Independence Day, the Phillies moved in with the Philadelphia A's on this date, splitting its doubleheader with the Boston Bees (5-10, 10-2).

With Baker Bowl aging, and costs of upkeep mounting, the Phils chose to share the rent with the A's in the newer, roomier, Shibe Park. They shared the tenancy up until the 1955 season, when the A's bolted for Kansas City.

5th

1953—In 2010, Roy Halladay led the Phillies and the league with nine complete games. In 1953, Robin Roberts pitched his 28th *straight* complete game, in a stretch that dated back to the previous season. Roberts got the shutout 2-0 victory over the Pittsburgh Pirates to earn his 13th win of the season.

Just another comparison—Cy Young runner-up Chris Carpenter *started 28 games in all* in 2009. Just three of them were complete games.

6th

1918—Sometimes "almost" is amazing enough. On this date, the Phillies *almost* completed the biggest single-game comeback in baseball history, losing 10-9 to the Cincinnati Reds.

Down 10-0 entering the ninth inning, the Phils had managed just one base hit off Cincy hurler Pete Schneider. Schneider then walked the inning's first six Philly batters, and nine runs had crossed the plate two relief pitchers later.

From nearly a one-hit complete game blowout, to a 10-9 squeaker in one inning. That's pretty amazing. Almost.

7th

1964—Following a 7-4 National League win in the Mid-Summer Classic, Phillies outfielder Johnny Callison was awarded the franchise's only All-Star Game MVP Award. His walk-off three-run home run in the bottom of the ninth inning, off Boston Red Sox pitcher Dick Radatz, earned him the honor on a team that included Hall of Famers Roberto Clemente, Willie Mays, Hank Aaron, Willie Stargell, and Orlando Cepeda.

Said Callison of the honor:

That homer was the greatest thrill of my life, but I remember thinking that it was only the beginning. It was going to be the Phillies' year. We had everything going our way. Everything.

Callison's clutch home run blast.
(AP Photo)

Everything had gone the Phillies' way up until that point. By the season's end, however, they would blow a six-and-a-half lead with 12 to play, to fall a game shy of reaching what would have been just the third World Series appearance for the 77-year-old franchise (see September 30th).

8th

1902—Philadelphia A's second baseman Danny Murphy was historically fashionably late.

Murphy's contract was just purchased from the minor league Norwich Reds the previous day, and he did not arrive at Boston's Huntington Avenue Grounds until the second frame of the ballgame—his debut with Philadelphia. Better late than never, Murphy went six for six in the contest (including a home run off Cy Young), having had no batting practice.

Library of Congress

The 22-9 win over the Boston Americans featured a 12-run sixth inning by the A's, and 45 total hits combined to set an American League record.

9th

1933—After a two-year absence from the NFL, Philadelphia had reacquired a team. On this date in '33, the Frankford

Yellow Jackets, which folded due to poor attendance, sold its territorial rights to Bert Bell and Lud Wray, and the Philadelphia Eagles were born.

Since only the rights to field a team in the Philadelphia market changed hands, the NFL treats the Yellow Jackets and Eagles as two separate teams.

10th

1911—Sherry Magee, one of the league's premier hitters at the time, knocked out umpire Bill Finneran after being ejected for arguing balls and strikes. His season-ending suspension was shortened to just 36 games after appeal.

Despite his misstep, Magee typically did most of his damage against opposing National League pitchers. In 1910, he led the Phils, and league, in batting average, RBI, and runs scored. (*Bain News Service*)

Skipper Jose Offerman slugged umpire Daniel Rayburn in a Dominican League game in 2010, and received a lifetime ban.

11th

1971—Deron Johnson of the Phillies clubbed his fourth home run in a row, in an 11-5 win over the Montreal Expos. Johnson used a homer in his final at-bat the previous day, and three on this date to tie the Major League record.

Three Phillies have hit four homers in a single game (see July 13th).

12th

1946—First baseman Vance Dinges hit the first, and only, pinch-hit inside-the-park home run in Phillies history. But it wasn't enough in a loss to the Pittsburgh Pirates, 4-3.

The lone bright spot of a brief 501-at-bat career, Dinges's accomplishment proves that all it takes is one swing to cement a legacy in America's pastime.

13th

1896—The nineteenth century is certainly not known in Major League Baseball as a sluggers' era, but on this date, Phillies outfielder Ed Delahanty accomplished an all-time home run feat.

In an 8-9 loss to the Chicago Colts, Delahanty hit four home runs in a single contest. Just the second player to do so (Bobby Lowe did it first for the Boston Beaneaters in 1894), Delahanty's mark, although currently shared by 15 other players, remains the only one accomplished with four inside-the-park homers.

COLOR COMMENTARY

Delahanty is one of three Phillies to hit four home runs in a game—Mike Schmidt and Chuck Klein being the others. Klein hit his four-in-one just three days shy of the 40th anniversary of Delahanty's big day, and Schmidt did it in April of 1976, 40 years after that. So, naturally, sometime in 2016, Domonic Brown is due for a big game.

14th

1988—Slugging his 537th career home run in a 7-5 Phillies loss to the Houston Astros, Mike Schmidt moved past Mickey Mantle for seventh place on the all-time home run list.

Since, Schmidt's spot in line has been going in reverse, getting passed by eight other sluggers, several of whom have been associated with the ongoing steroids controversy.

15th

1991—Sandra Ortiz-Del Valle became the first female official of a men's professional basketball game, in a United States Basketball League (USBL) game between the New Haven Skyhawks and Philadelphia Spirit.

The USBL, a now-defunct professional spring league, crowned the Philly Spirit league champions in '91, the team's first season (of just two) in the league.

2007—A 10-2 regular season loss to the St. Louis Cardinals by the eventual NL East winner wouldn't normally be newsworthy. But when it's loss number 10,000 in team history, far and away more than any other professional franchise, it's a big deal—but the Phillies had nowhere to go but up.

By season's end, the Fightins had their first division crown in 14 years.

16th

2003—The 76ers inked Kenny Thomas to a seven-year $50 million contract. The shocking move was a lesson learned for Philadelphia and the league, in an age where cap strength means everything and (very) long-term deals routinely end in disappointment. Thomas' production immediately declined following his payday, enticing the team to trade him in a package for Chris Webber, whose own cap number crippled the team financially until the 2008 season.

COLOR COMMENTARY

Thomas' seven-season pact was actually one of the last contracts of its kind in league history. Jamal Crawford, with the New York Knicks, signed the NBA's final seven-year deal in 2004. Under the current collective bargaining agreement, teams cannot sign a player beyond five seasons.

17th

1918—The Phillies played the longest game (innings-wise) in team history, losing 2-1 to the Chicago Cubs in 21 innings. But both bullpens stayed well-rested because, well, they hadn't really been invented yet.

Both starting pitchers went the distance in the contest, Chicago's Lefty Tyler taking the win over Philly's Milt Watson. Giving up a run apiece in the game's first and final frame, Watson pitched 19 straight scoreless innings.

18th

1927—Ty Cobb, a 22-year veteran with the Detroit Tigers, got his 4,000th Major League base hit on this date, in a Philadelphia Athletics uniform.

Fittingly, Cobb reached the milestone against his former club, earning a double in the 5-3 loss to Detroit. He was the first player to reach the milestone, part of a club that now includes just Cobb and Pete Rose.

1954—A brawl broke out in the first inning of a game between the Phillies and St. Louis Cardinals at Busch Stadium, significantly delaying the game's progress. Because a Major League Baseball game cannot be constituted as final until the completion of the fifth inning, the Cards began to stall as the sixth frame drew near.

Down 8-1 in the fifth inning of an unusually long game, the Cardinals were stalling and brawling to take advantage of two rules:

1. A Major League Baseball game cannot be constituted as final until the completion of the fifth inning.
2. Due to a local ordinance, the lights cannot be turned on to continue a ball game.

Fortunately for the Phils, the umpires halted the Cards' filibuster, awarding a forfeit victory to Philadelphia.

In the record books, the game is recorded as a 0-0 St. Louis forfeiture.

19th

1960—Hall of Famer Juan Marichal, of the San Francisco Giants, made his Major League debut on this date, tossing a one-hit shutout gem against the Phillies. The Phils' rookie pinch hitter, Clay Dalrymple, mustered the only hit off of the Dominican Dandy.

It was the first of 243 wins of Marichal's illustrious career.

20th

1958—Dow Finsterwald won the 40th PGA Championship at Llanerch Country Club in Havertown, Pennsylvania.

Finsterwald finished at four under par, two strokes ahead of Billy Casper, and four strokes ahead of third-place finisher and the PGA Tour's all-time wins leader, Sam Snead.

It was the first PGA Championship under current modern stroke play rules, and the only major held at Llanerch.

21st

1892—In June of 1986, two 300-game winners faced each other, with Don Sutton taking the hill for California in the Angels' 9-3 victory over Phil Niekro and the Cleveland Indians.

The only time two 300-game winners squared off prior to that matchup?

This dates all the way back to 1892, when the Phillies' Tim Keefe bested Jim "Pud" Galvin of the St. Louis Browns, 2-0.

The feat wouldn't be matched in the National League again until 2005, with the Chicago Cubs' Greg Maddux out-dueling the Houston Astros' Roger Clemens, 3-2.

22nd

1955—With a 6-3 win over the St. Louis Cardinals, the Phillies had won their 11th straight home game, the longest home streak in consecutive games in franchise history.

The 11-game run, the team's longest overall win streak since 1892 (franchise record, 16 games), followed a 13-game *losing* streak in May.

23rd

1965—The Phils' Dick Stuart homered at Shea Stadium, in a 5-1 win over the New York Mets, to become the first player in Major League history to hit a home run in 23 ballparks.

Stuart, however, is best remembered for his nickname, *Dr. Strangelove*, mocking his abysmal defensive play. He led or tied for the league lead in errors his first seven years in baseball.

1978—Steve Carlton, four-time Cy Young winner with the Phillies, became the 78th person in Major League Baseball to win 200 games, in a 13-2 victory over the Houston Astros.

24th

2002—In one of the best rookie debuts in Phillies history, 21-year-old Brett Myers, almost three years to the day he signed his first professional contract, two-hit the Chicago Cubs through eight innings to collect the win in a 4-2 Phils victory.

25th

2001—The first sports trainer to ascend to an ownership position with a professional sports franchise (with majority partners Ed Snider and Comcast Corporation), Pat Croce was a living success story and fiery sparkplug that changed attitudes and transformed the last-place moribund 76ers franchise into a title contender within five years. On this day in 2001, after a whirlwind playoff run to the NBA Finals, Croce stepped down as president of the team. And while Croce's absence would be far-fetched to blame for the team's decade-long struggles, there's something to be said for a lack of publicly perceived positive influence.

2015—Cole Hamels threw the 13th no-hitter in franchise history. The 5-0 blanking of the Cubs was Hamels's final start with the club before a trade deadline deal that landed the left-hander in Texas.

(Kevin Durso)

When asked where the outing ranks among his career accomplishments, Hamels said, "Nothing will top winning a World Series, but this is right under it."

Hamels is the first and only pitcher to change teams in-season following a no-hitter.

26th

2000—Phils GM Ed Wade traded Curt Schilling to the Arizona Diamondbacks on this date, receiving four, ultimately fruitless, players in return—Travis Lee, Omar Daal, Vicente Padilla, and Nelson Figueroa.

Schilling and Randy Johnson formed the most dynamic pitching duo of the decade, winning the World Series the following year for the D-Backs.

COLOR COMMENTARY

Lee and Daal were both scrubs (and Figueroa never made a big MLB impact). Those guys were merely space fillers, but Padilla had some staying power.

Padilla actually made the All-Star team in 2002. Most importantly, though, while pitching for the Dodgers, he gave up the deciding runs in a Game 5 NLCS Phillies victory, launching the team into its second straight World Series. That's got to count for something.

What stings is that Schilling was a critical cog in the D-Backs (2001) and Boston Red Sox (2004, 2007) championship runs. His career took a potential Hall of Fame turn with his post-Phillies postseason dominance. The 2008 title lessens the pain, but, really, the Phils should have gotten more for Schill.

27th

2008—The Philadelphia Soul defeated the San Jose Saber-Cats, 59-56, in the Arena Football League's ArenaBowl XXII.

Despite a return to play in 2010, the league final was the last in the original AFL's history. The current incarnation is actually that of the upstart Arena Football 1, operating under the veil of the defunct league's trademarks.

Shortly after the 2008 Arena Bowl, financial difficulties led to the sudden fold of the New Orleans VooDoo franchise, in what proved to be foreshadowing for the fate of the league entirely. At auction, the AFL and its assets were sold off to AF1, fielding 15 teams originally, and only recently luring the Soul franchise back into the fray.

The Soul finished as runner up to the Arizona Rattlers in both ArenaBowl XXV (72-54), and XXVI (48-39).

28th

1875—Joe Borden, of the Philadelphia White Stockings, hurled the first recorded no-hitter in professional baseball, in a 4-0 blanking of Chicago's White Stockings.

The Philadelphia White Stockings—also called the Pearls or even Phillies—could generally be considered Philly's first pro ball club, competing in the National Association of Professional Base Ball Players (NAPBBP), the nation's first attempt at organizing a professional league. While the White Stockings (1873–75) were short lived, the league itself (1871–75) was trounced only by the tides of progress, dissolving into the National League in 1876, which thrives today.

2002—Legendary Phillies broadcaster Harry Kalas received the prestigious Ford C. Frick award from the National Baseball Hall of Fame in Cooperstown, New York. Awarded annually to a broadcaster demonstrating "major contributions to baseball," it is the profession's highest honor, on par with a player's induction into the Hall itself.

Kalas, ever the crowd pleaser, dedicated most of his acceptance speech to thanking the Philadelphia fans. In fact, he even recited an original poem dedicated to the Philly faithful.

29th

2002—Scott Rolen, All-Star face of the Phillies (and allegedly a team "cancer," according to an anonymous teammate), forced a trade to the St. Louis Cardinals, ending a tumultuous relationship with ownership, spurned by Rolen's public scrutiny of the team's commitment to winning. The Phillies received reliever Mike Timlin (who bolted for free agency at season's end), former no-hit hurling lefty Bud Smith (who would soon become a Minor League mainstay), and infielder Placido Polanco (who would be traded nearly three years later for Ugeuth Urbina, who later served time in a Venezuelan prison).

At the surface, it was an uneven trade. But with franchise cornerstones Chase Utley, Ryan Howard, and Cole Hamels waiting in the wings, the "cancer" had been cut, and good things were soon to come.

Polanco would resume the hot corner in Philadelphia in 2010.

30th

1995—Two of the most beloved Philadelphia Phillies of all time, Mike Schmidt and Richie Ashburn, were inducted into the National Baseball Hall of Fame in Cooperstown, NY, in front of nearly 28,000 fans, mostly clad in red.

Schmidt garnered 96.5% of the BBWAA's 460 ballots on his first try, finishing his career in many minds as the greatest third baseman in baseball history. Ashburn, selected by the Veterans Committee, after too long of a wait, was a lifetime .308 hitter, a two-time batting champion, and a beloved Phillies broadcaster for more than 30 years.

COLOR COMMENTARY

I don't remember if there was a more beautiful day than this one. An absolutely gorgeous sun-splashed afternoon in central New York.

There I was amongst a sea of red, basking in the glorious sunshine, and beaming with pride witnessing the induction of two Philadelphia legends in front of a record crowd.

The speeches were tremendous. Schmidt made peace with the Philadelphia fans as well as stumping for Pete Rose and his plight for induction (we're still waiting). And Ashburn's was just wonderful, saying hello to his mother in the front row, and filling up with emotion as he closed with "...thank you for making this the greatest day of my life."

No Richie, thank you, my friend, and Michael Jack. You gave Philadelphians joy and happiness for a long time. That was, and still is to this day, one of my favorite sports road trips ever.

2006—In a salary dump, Phillies GM Pat Gillick traded Bobby Abreu, a member of the All-Vet Stadium Team, to the New York Yankees (along with Cory Lidle) in exchange for C. J. Henry, Carlos Monasterios, Jesus Sanchez, and Matt Smith.

The four prospects managed, in total, just 12 2/3 Major League innings pitched for Philadelphia (all from lefty reliever Matt Smith).

31st

1994—Steve Carlton, arguably Philadelphia's greatest hurler, was inducted into the Baseball Hall of Fame on this date, along with Yankees great Phil Rizzuto.

Lefty was the first pitcher to win four Cy Young awards (currently third-most in history). He is the Phillies' all-time leader in games started, wins, and strikeouts, and was ranked no. 26 on ESPN's *Hall of 100* list of the 100 greatest baseball players of all time.

1st

1945—Irv Hall, a light-hitting shortstop with the Philadelphia Athletics, is barely a blip on the radar in baseball history, batting just .261 in four seasons. But an ultimately meaningless single in a loss to the Washington Senators (1-2) helps his name live on.

On this date, Hall hit Washington pitcher Dutch Leonard with a line drive. Striking the pitcher in the stomach, the ball lodged itself in Leonard's pants (sports' first wardrobe malfunction?) and Hall was credited with a single.

1950—Phillies left-hander Curt Simmons became the first Major League player to be called into active military duty during the Korean War. He won 17 games for Philadelphia during his war-shortened 1950 campaign, and was sorely missed in the World Series, as the New York Yankees swept the Phils in four games.

2nd

2013—Prior to Philadelphia's 6-4 loss to the Atlanta Braves, Curt Schilling was honored and inducted into the Phillies Wall of Fame. A tradition since 1978, and including Philadelphia Athletics Alumni until 2003, Schilling was the 60th member to join the Wall.

Schilling, arguably the team's greatest right-handed power pitcher, won 101 games (sixth-best in franchise history) and struck out 1,554 batters (fourth-best) for Philadelphia. Before his postseason heroics earned him three World Series rings for other teams (Arizona Diamondbacks, 2001; Boston Red Sox, 2003/2007), Schilling shut out the Toronto Blue Jays 2-0 in

Game 5 of the 1993 Series, one of the strongest performances in club history.

3rd

1949—The Basketball Association of America (BAA) and National Basketball League (NBL) merged to create the National Basketball Association (NBA). The Philadelphia Warriors of the BAA, from this point forward, would play in the same league as the Syracuse Nationals (Philadelphia 76ers) of the NBL.

On March 23, 1950, the Nationals defeated the Warriors, 59-53, to complete the two-game sweep of the first NBA playoff series for either team.

2003—The first ticketed event, a football game, was played at Lincoln Financial Field, but it wasn't an Eagles game, and nor was it a college football matchup. Actually, it wasn't even football—not American football anyway. A soccer match between Manchester United and FC Barcelona kicked off the action at the Eagles' and Temple Owls' new home.

4th

1933—Right-hander Flint Rhem allowed the most earned runs in Phillies recorded history, surrendering 15 earned, and 16 runs in all, through eight innings of an 18-2 loss to the New York Giants. Rhem's outing was bad, but it wasn't the worst.

In 2015, Phillies starter David Buchanan took a run at the worst start in team history, amongst pitchers with at least 1 complete inning. He surrendered 11 earned runs in just 1.2

innings of work against the Arizona Diamondbacks. His 59.42 ERA that game was much higher than Rhem's (16.88), but Buchanan's outing is narrowly spared from the dubious distinction—Hugh Mulcahy surrendered 10 earned runs in 1.1 innings of work against the Giants in 1940, for a 67.52 ERA.

1947—Perhaps the greatest lightweight rivalry in Philadelphia boxing history, Jersey native Ike Williams settled the score against Philadelphia's own Bob Montgomery, by way of a sixth-round knockout.

Three years earlier, Williams was on the losing end to Montgomery, but this bout, in front of 30,501 fans at Philadelphia's Municipal/JFK Stadium, had much more on the line. Both holding a piece of the 135-pound title (Montgomery, king of the ring in New York and Philly; Williams, the National Boxing Association champ), Williams evened the heated series against his sworn enemy.

2015—It was a celebration of old and new at Citizens Bank Park. Jimmy Rollins made his first return to Philadelphia as a member of the LA Dodgers, and Phils rookie Maikel Franco made sure it was a happy one for the home team.

Rollins went 2-for-5 at the plate, but Franco stole the show, hitting a grand slam in the 7th inning, scoring the deciding runs of the Phils' 6-2 win. Franco was the first rookie since Ryan Howard in 2005 to hit a grand slam for the Fightins.

5th

1921—KDKA in Pittsburgh, the nation's first commercially licensed radio station, broadcasted radio's first baseball game, an 8-5 Phillies loss to the Pittsburgh Pirates.

GCC, circa 1978. (*Library of Congress*)

The Phillies didn't have their own exclusive broadcast team until 1950, with announcers Bill Brundige and Gene Kelly for WPEN.

1938—At the 33rd Davis Cup, the United States defeated Australia, 3-2. It was the last Davis Cup tournament to be held at the Germantown Cricket Club (GCC) in Philadelphia.

Today, the Davis Cup is the premier men's team tennis spectacle, and among the most prestigious international team events in all of sports—and Philadelphia was among the event's early hosts. The US had a 4-1 overall record in the City of Brotherly Love, winning in its first three years at the GCC (1924–26).

6th

1963—The team formerly known as the Syracuse Nationals selected a winner in its contest to rename Philadelphia's newest NBA team. Among hundreds of entries, New Jersey resident Walt Stahlberg won, coining the franchise the "76ers" to commemorate the city's part in the signing of the Declaration of Independence in 1776. The adopted condensed version, the "Sixers," was first popularized by local beat writers.

2012—In a 6-1 loss to the Atlanta Braves, the Phillies, collectively, had struck out zero times (small victories).

To date (the start of the 2016 season), it is the Phillies' only no-strikeout game since Opening Day of the 2011 season. By comparison, the Cincinnati Reds have struck out at least once in every game dating back to June of 1997—the same month Cornelius Randolph, the team's top draft pick in 2015, was born.

7th

2000—GM Ed Wade made perhaps the most confusing, convoluted deal of his Phillies career.

Trading Mickey Morandini to the Toronto Blue Jays, the Phils got Rob Ducey in return—a player Wade had traded *to* Toronto just 12 days earlier. Essentially, the Phils traded Morandini for John Sneed (the player received in the original deal), while Ducey was swapped for *himself*.

8th

1903—During a game at the Phillies' Baker Bowl on this date, a raucous disturbance taking place just outside the stadium stole the attention of fans in the left field bleachers. The excess weight of fans gathering toward the highest end of the left field seating collapsed the section of wooden bleachers, killing 12 and injuring 232 others.

The event, which became a black mark on the Phillies organization, forced team owner John Rogers to sell the team to James Potter after an ensuing onslaught of lawsuits.

An article in *The Star* (Wilmington, DE, August 9th, 1903) described the scene: "The sight was one never to be forgotten, and one which Philadelphians never before witnessed. In every direction the wounded were being borne upon stretchers, or mattresses borrowed from nearby dwellings, while others lay moaning with pain upon the baseball diamond awaiting assistance."

2009—Philadelphia, an early adopter of the X Games and pro wrestling events, has never been shy to host the latest evolutions in sports and entertainment. Such was the case on this date, as the Ultimate Fighting Championship (UFC), the world's premiere mixed martial arts event, stopped in Philly for the first time.

The UFC 101 event generated a live gate of $3.55 million, the largest for a fight card in PA history, according to *Philadelphia Daily News* boxing guru Bernard Fernandez.

B. J. Penn won the main event by submission over Kenny Florian, but the story of the event was the fans that came out in droves.

"Philly," wrote John Gonzalez of the *Inquirer*, "did for the UFC and its athletes what it did for boxing for so many years—bestowed legitimacy and importance on the event."

9th

1919—On this date, the Phillies traded Possum Whitted to the Pittsburgh Pirates for future Hall of Famer Casey Stengel.

And while Stengel would hit a respectable .284 over a 14-year playing career spent mostly with the Brooklyn Robins, he was inducted into the Hall of Fame as a coach in 1966, winning seven titles as skipper of the New York Yankees.

A fun piece of trivia relevant to Stengel: in 1921, the Phillies had two players on their roster who would go on to be

Hall of Fame coaches—one in baseball (Stengel), and one in football.

Outfielder Greasy Neale, coach of the 1948–49 NFL Champion Eagles, was the other.

10th

1974—The ironically named Jorge *Lebron,* at just 14 years of age, became the youngest professional ballplayer in history.

The Phillies signed the Puerto Rican little leaguer in July of 1974 to play for their minor league affiliate, the Auburn Phillies. Doomed from the start, due to child labor laws, lack of production, and unrealistic expectations, the young infielder's career ended after just three seasons.

1981—Phillies first baseman Pete Rose got his 3,631st hit in a 7-3 loss to the St. Louis Cardinals, to tie Cards alum Stan Musial (who was attending the game) for the most in National League history. Hank Aaron (3,771), currently third on the NL list, would have passed Musial himself if not for a trade to the American League's Milwaukee Brewers, robbing him of 171 possible NL hits.

11th

1950—The 1949 NFL Champion Eagles lost to the College All-Stars, 17-7, in the Chicago Charities College All-Star Game. The summer spectacle, played from 1934 to 1976, pitted the league's defending champion (or Super Bowl champion, when applicable) against a squad of all-star college seniors.

Charlie Justice, College Football Hall of Fame running back for North Carolina, was the MVP of the game, which was played in front of 88,885 people at Soldier Field.

2004—Randy Wolf became just the seventh pitcher in Phillies history to hit two home runs in the same game.

Wolf picked up three RBI while surrendering four runs over seven innings in a 15-4 win over the Rockies at Citizens Bank Park. He also singled in the game, becoming the first Phillies pitcher since Phil Collins in 1930 to amass nine total bases in a single contest.

12th

1993—Moses Malone, hero of the 1983 Sixers championship team and "Fo', fo', fo'" prognosticator, re-signed with Philadelphia, if only to be the on-court tutor of the Sixers' 7'6" draft pick, Shawn Bradley.

Malone, 38 at the time, was way past his prime and in way

over his head trying to turn the rail-thin Bradley into a viable post presence. While Malone stuck around long enough to reach the third spot on the NBA's all-time scoring list by season's end (27,360), Bradley did little to earn his keep as one of the team's prolific draft busts (see June 30th).

(AP Photo)

13th

1972—Phillies VP Bill Giles contracted circus performer Karl Wallenda, 67, to tight-rope walk across the middle of Veterans Stadium between games of a doubleheader.

The world-famous Wallenda completed the stunt (while Giles was having second thoughts), but, with paying customers sitting directly below, it's unlikely you'll ever see something like this today.

14th

1997—On this date, the Flyers made an all-time regrettable (and expensive) free agent signing.

With Eric Lindros and John LeClair flourishing in their primes, the third leg of the "Legion of Doom" line, winger Mikael Renberg, was beginning a swift decline. Looking for a chance to upgrade, the Flyers jumped at the opportunity to sign restricted free agent Chris Gratton, former no. 3 overall draft pick in 1993 and 30-goal scorer in '96–'97, from the Tampa Bay Lightning. And while he performed respectably in '97–'98, registering 62 points in 82 games, he scored just one goal through 26 games for Philadelphia the following season before being shipped back to Tampa via trade.

The Flyers gave Gratton a $9 million signing bonus and surrendered Renberg and Karl Dykhuis to the Lightning in the deal. And although Renberg returned to Philadelphia in the *take-back* trade with Tampa, it remains a prime example of GM Bobby Clarke's misplaced aggression during the Flyers' late-'90s surge.

2001—One of the final embarrassing black marks on the Vet Stadium turf, the first field condition–related NFL cancellation in six years occurred on this date between the Eagles and Baltimore Ravens. Uneven cuts caused the field to be deemed unplayable, and team president Joe Banner vented his frustration with the on-the-outs Veterans Stadium to the media:"We're disappointed. We've been going through this for years. It's not acceptable. The conditions this team is forced to play in is absolutely unacceptable and an embarrassment to the city of Philadelphia."

15th

1990—Terry Mulholland, a lefty starter for the Phillies, tossed the first no-hitter in Vet Stadium history, and the only no-no at home for the Phils in the 1900s, facing the minimum 27 batters in a 6-0 win over the San Francisco Giants. Mulholland played for 11 teams during a Major League career that spanned more than 20 years.

16th

1968—The enigmatic Richie Allen, among the Phillies' greatest all-time power hitters, kept the bat on his shoulders on this date, drawing a National League record–tying five walks in a single game in a 7-5 loss to the LA Dodgers.

Allen, as recognized for his surly attitude as he was for his 351 career home runs, won the National League Rookie of the Year award in 1964, and the MVP for the Chicago White Sox in 1972.

It has been widely speculated that character issues alone have kept the seven-time All-Star out of the Hall of Fame.

17th

2001—The Summer X Games landed in Philadelphia for the first time. The ground-breaking extreme sports competition took a rare trip East (Los Angeles hosted the event for 11 straight years after Philly went back-to-back in 2002). 235,000 fans showed up for the week-long event, ESPN's seventh installment of the extreme sports pinnacle.

18th

1909—The colorful Arlie Latham, nicknamed "The Freshest Man on Earth," became the oldest player (49) in Major League Baseball history to steal a base, swiping second for the New York Giants in a 14-1 win over the Phillies.

Latham, right, as player/coach for the 1909 Giants (*Bain News Service*)

One of baseball's most zany characters, Latham was famous for running up and down the baselines as a third base coach, while yelling obscenities to opposing pitchers to distract them.

One of his players during his coaching days with the Giants once commented years later that Latham "was probably the worst third base coach that ever lived."

2015–76ers center Joel Embiid underwent bone-graft surgery on his right foot, ending his 2015-16 season before it began. It was the second foot procedure for Embiid, who missed the entirety of the 2014-15 season with the same ailment—which was preceded by recurring back issues in college.

In retrospect, the red flags surrounding Embiid should have been as radiant and distinct as a peacock's tail—even the 7-foot center himself thought he might slip to the second round of the 2014 NBA Draft. Instead, the Sixers took Embiid third overall, gaining little to date other than hard-learned lessons.

19th

2006—Speaking of older players... Jamie Moyer, a native of Sellersville, PA, was acquired from the Seattle Mariners.

Moyer, 43 at the time, had pitched most of his 20 seasons in the majors with Seattle, twice compiling 20-win seasons while leading the Mariners staff. His most rewarding season, though, came with the Phillies in 2008, as the crafty left-hander, at 45 years young, won 16 games with a 3.71 ERA while earning his first World Series championship ring.

COLOR COMMENTARY

In my ten-plus seasons as a member of the Philadelphia media, I have met many athletes who have come and gone through this town. There have been many interesting personalities, but very few who have been as pleasant, genuine, and down to earth as Jamie Moyer.

One evening, after a Phillies win in 2008, I sat with Jamie for about an hour. The clubhouse had long emptied out, but we continued our chat on baseball, parenting, Philadelphia, charity, etc. It was, for me, a very enlightening hour, and a moment that will forever be one of my career favorites.

2015—On the eight-month anniversary of the trade that sent shortstop Jimmy Rollins to the Dodgers, the Phillies dealt J-Roll's longtime double-play partner Chase Utley to LA, as well.

The pair formed, arguably, the best middle infield combo in Phillies team history, playing together from 2003-14. Rollins leads all Phillies shortstops in WAR (Wins Above Replacement; 46.1), and Utley leads all Phils second basemen (61.5), trailing only Mike Schmidt (106.5) for the top spot in franchise history.

The Phillies received outfielder Darnell Sweeney and pitcher John Richy in the deal. Sweeney, 24, batted just .176 in 37 games for the Phillies in 2015.

20th

1961—This day in Phillies history will be remembered for setting and ending a dubious team record.

In Game 1 of a doubleheader, the Phils lost to the Milwaukee Braves, 5-2, extending its team-record losing streak to an astonishing 23 games.

In Game 2, the streak was finally snapped in a 7-4 win. Before the win, Philadelphia was 1-28 in their previous 29, and had managed separate losing streaks on the season of ten, eight, and seven games. They finished the year in last place at 47-107.

On the year, Hall of Famer Robin Roberts was 1-10, while three other Phillies starting pitchers lost at least 16 games (Art Mahaffey, 19; John Buzhardt, 18; Frank Sullivan, 16). Of the offensive starters, only Tony Gonzalez (.277) hit over .266.

21st

1883—The Quakers (founded in 1883, the Phillies' original, though vaguely unofficial, moniker was the Quakers) wasted no time securing their worst all-time defeat, falling to the Providence Grays on this day, 28-0, in their very first season.

The Phils finished their inaugural season at 17-81, fielding a team that was, according to Rich Westcott and Frank Bilovsky, authors of *The Phillies Encyclopedia*, "made up mostly of ex-minor leaguers and players they were able to coax away from other National League teams."

22nd

1926—Owner/Manager Connie Mack and his Philadelphia Athletics defeated the Chicago White Sox, 3-2, in Philadelphia's first—though illegal—Sunday baseball game.

Philly's "Blue Laws" prevented professional sports from being played on the day of rest and worship, but the authorities were powerless to make an arrest. Through fortunate loopholes, the "breach of peace" could not be proven until the event had actually taken place, so the police could not prevent it. And after the contest had gone on without a hitch or disturbance, the best Philadelphia officials could do was wait until Monday to prosecute—with a penalty of just six days in jail OR a $4 fine.

The test game is not listed in team history as an official contest.

23rd

1992—On very rare occasions, a pitcher will hurl a no-hitter and lose. Rarer still, one no-hit pitcher will win and one will lose, in the same game.

Two minor league teams, The Clearwater Phillies and Winter Haven Red Sox, hurled a *double no-hitter* on this date. Andy Carter of the Phils and Scott Bakkum of the Sox both held the opposition hitless through nine innings.

Who won? Two walks and two sacrifice bunts swayed the game in the Phils' favor, as Carter picked up the unique victory for Clearwater, 1-0.

24th

1983—The Philadelphia Arena, the original home of the Philadelphia Warriors and 76ers basketball teams, was destroyed by arson on this date. A do-it-all venue in its day, the Arena hosted boxing cards, professional hockey games... even rodeos.

COLOR COMMENTARY

I've always felt this was a much more logical "curse" of Philadelphia's pro sports teams than the adopted Billy Penn statue hex. Considering the historical building was mysteriously destroyed (arson?) just a couple months following the Sixers' 1983 championship, the timeline seemed right for the dawn of a 25-year championship drought.

25th

1965—The city's greatest individual rivalry, Wilt Chamberlain and Bill Russell were always looking to one-up the other.

On this date, Russell, literally, got *one dollar up* on Chamberlain, signing with the Boston Celtics for a single bill more than the Big Dipper. The contract was for $100,001 per year.

26th

2008—The Phillies completed a crucial comeback victory on this date, in a turning point game of their eventual championship season.

Down 7-0 in the fourth inning to the first-place New York Mets, the Phillies scored seven unanswered runs of their own, including a two-out RBI double by Eric Bruntlett in the ninth. Chris Coste then added a walk-off RBI single in the 13th to seal the victory for Philadelphia and position the Phils atop the NL East . . . for one day anyway.

The Mets would immediately take back the lead atop the NL East standings—a lead the Phils would not reclaim until the very last game of the regular season (see September 30th).

27th

2000—Breaking a 1-1 tie in the bottom of the 10th inning at the Vet, Bobby Abreu hit a walk-off home run, of the *inside the park* variety.

Abreu was responsible for all of the scoring in the Phils' 2-1 win over the San Francisco Giants, slugging a conventional home run to lead off the sixth.

According to baseball-reference.com, Abreu is one of just 15 players with inside-the-park walk-offs since 1950, joining Phillies Bobby Dernier and the duo of Johnny Callison and Richie Allen, who, a year apart, both hit theirs off of Houston Astros pitcher Jim Owens.

COLOR COMMENTARY

There are certain memories from being a sports fan in Philadelphia, and these walk-off inside-the-park home runs (Dernier, then Abreu) rank right up there. I suppose it's because they are such a rarity, but for me it's the combination of the thrill of victory and the ability to listen to the call over and over.

I attended the game in which Abreu conquered this feat, but I recall Dernier's as being more magical. If you have a spare moment, relive them both on YouTube. It's worth it every time.

28th

1918—League officials notified the Cleveland Indians they would be without their best player for the remaining five games of the season.

Cleveland's Tris Speaker was ejected the previous day during an 8-6 win over the Athletics in Philadelphia after reportedly assaulting the home plate umpire, Tom Connolly, during a late game tussle.

Though it seems, oddly, like a slap on the wrist, Major League Baseball did not come down as hard on players then as they do now. Babe Ruth earned a similar penalty after punching an umpire in 1917.

In 2006 however, Tampa Bay Devil Rays prospect Delmon Young received a *50-game* suspension for tossing his bat at an umpire in an international league game.

29th

1885—Charlie Ferguson, of the Quakers, hurled the first no-hitter in Phillies history on this date (Quakers/Phillies, see August 21st).

Ferguson, Philadelphia's best hurler in the early days, won 99 games for the team in a career shortened by his untimely death in 1888.

The Quakers won the game, 1-0, against the Providence Grays.

30th

1913—On this date, the Phillies began a nine-inning game that wouldn't be completed for two months.

Umpire William Brennan awarded a forfeit victory to the New York Giants over the Phillies, after Philly fans were relentless in their distracting taunts of Giants hitters.

The Phils had an 8-6 lead in the ninth inning when the game was called, a major contributing factor to National League President Thomas Lynch overturning the forfeiture and awarding the

Ferguson, 1887 Old Judge (N172). (*Library of Congress*)

victory to Philadelphia three days later. But it wouldn't end there.

Subsequently, an MLB panel ordered the game to be played to its completion from the time it was halted, and on October 2, the Phils got the remaining two outs in the game and earned the victory, without protest.

New York had the last laugh though, winning the pennant by 12.5 games over second-place Philadelphia.

31st

2003—With a perfect 10-0 record, Team USA won the gold at the 2003 FIBA Americas Olympic Qualifying Men's Basketball Tournament in Puerto Rico (106-73).

The 76ers' Allen Iverson was the second-leading scorer, contributing 14.3 points per game, on a team led by Larry Brown, who had resigned as head coach of the Sixers two months earlier. Ultimately, the team is remembered more for its failures in the 2004 Olympic Games in Greece.

Team USA lost to Argentina (a team they handled in the FIBA tournament), 89-81, in the semifinals before settling for the bronze. The three leading scorers for the US in the loss were Stephon Marbury, Lamar Odom, and Iverson.

Not exactly a "Dream Team."

1st

1991—Eagles quarterback Randall Cunningham was the one on the ground, writhing—but Eagles fans everywhere were also feeling the pain.

It was Week 1 of the 1991 season, and the Birds were riding high on expectations brought on by the leadership of an elite defensive unit and the NFL's reigning MVP in Cunningham.

Then, just two quarters in, a Super Bowl run was squashed. Cunningham tore two ligaments in his knee to open the second quarter of play, on a hit from Bryce Paup of the Green Bay Packers. It spoke to the fragility of greatness, and the waning nature of golden opportunities. Ultimately, the Birds finished the season 10-6, using five different starting quarterbacks and anchored by one of the greatest defensive showings in NFL history, as they finished ranked no. 1 against the pass and run, as well as overall defense. They sent five players to the Pro Bowl on the defensive side, including three starters from the D-line alone—a feat matched just five times in league history.

While they certainly missed Cunningham, backup quarterback Jim McMahon collected the season's Comeback Player of the Year award.

2007—It happens all the time—a pitcher gets an incalculable "infinite" ERA, having allowed one or more runs without recording an out. On this date, J.D. Durbin surrendered the most earned runs in such an occurrence (7), pitching the most egregious single-game infinite ERA in team history. The first seven Marlins hitters reached base and scored off the rookie hurler, setting the stage for an easy 12-6 Florida victory.

2nd

1979—Part of a 23-17 victory over the New York Giants in Week 1 of the '79 NFL season, rookie placekicker Tony Franklin nailed the first *barefoot* field goal in Eagles history—a 46-yarder in the second quarter.

Franklin was one of just four known barefoot kickers in NFL history, and the first of two for the Eagles (Paul McFadden was the other).

3rd

1983—Marion Campbell succeeded Dick Vermeil as head coach of the Philadelphia Eagles, winning his first game, 22-17, over the San Francisco 49ers. The Eagles would go on to win three of their next five contests, but ultimately finish out the year at 5-11—the first of five straight sub-.500 seasons.

1995—"For who? For what?" posed Eagles running back and big free agent signing Ricky Watters. After his first game with Philadelphia, in which he fumbled twice and infamously short-armed a potential completion over the middle of the field, Watters began the season on the hot seat. And while Watters wondered aloud why he'd risk a big hit, Eagles fans gave him a reason, clogging the lines of local sports talk radio to voice their disapproval.

2000—In the first game of McNabb's first full season as the Eagles' starting quarterback, Philadelphia thwarted the Cowboys' best efforts with the help of an opening onside kick recovery.

Furthering the oddities, their reported sideline consumption of thirst-quenching pickle juice (to combat the scorching

109-degree Texas heat) led most national coverage of the game, which became known as "The Pickle Juice Game."

It was certainly a game of firsts for the franchise, and with the 41-17 win over the rival Cowboys, the team captured its first win of the season as well.

2006—Ryan Howard became the first player in Phillies history to belt 50 home runs in a season. In addition, he became the 17th Phillies player (of 18 to date, most recently including Jayson Werth) to hit three home runs in a single game, all of which came in his first three at-bats.

The feat, accomplished in an 8-7 win over the Atlanta Braves, pushed Howard's home run total to 52 (58 by season's end)—a Major League record among second-year players.

4th

1983—Jay Sigel, one of the most unique amateurs in the history of golf, won his second straight US Amateur Championship.

A native of Bryn Mawr and 2005 inductee into the Philadelphia Sports Hall of Fame, Sigel was just the eighth player in the tournament's 88-year history to accomplish the feat. And just a month later, he added the US Mid-Amateur to his trophy case, becoming the only golfer to capture both in the same year. What set him apart from the rest of the field was not just a superior talent, but a superior age.

Sigel, 39 at the time, captured the titles (and a runner-up in the Canadian Amateur that year, for good measure) while competing in a field comprised mostly of twenty-somethings, paying their obligatory dues with sights set primarily on PGA Tour payouts.

In 1994, at age 50, Sigel finally dropped his amateur status and joined the Senior PGA Tour/Champions Tour. To date, he has won eight events on the Tour, with over $9 million in career earnings.

5th

1971—New York Mets outfielder Don Hahn hit the first-ever inside-the-park home run at Veterans Stadium. Hahn, known mostly for his fielding prowess, ended his career with only eight round-trippers.

He was also a one-time Phillie, registering just five ABs in 1975, but more importantly, his arrival from a trade with the Mets also brought to town the beloved Tug McGraw.

6th

1998—The season opener for the Eagles happened to be against the Seattle Seahawks, to where Eagles former running back Ricky Watters had just departed via free agency. On this date, the Seahawks came out on top—way on top—winning 38-0 at the Vet. It was the first of a franchise-record 13 defeats for the Eagles, and also the worst home opener loss in team history.

7th

1911—Baseball's quintessential passing of the torch: 24-year-old future Hall of Famer Grover Cleveland Alexander (long before he earned the nickname "Ol' Pete") won his rookie-record 23rd game, in a 1-0 Phils win over the Boston Rustlers. Alexander, fittingly, earned the win against the pitching award namesake, Cy Young, age 44, in his final Major League season.

Alexander finished the season with 28 wins total.

8th

1998—In a 16-4 drubbing of the New York Mets, the Phillies clubbed a franchise-record seven home runs, with Rico Brogna, Kevin Sefcik, and Bobby Estalella each hitting two out, and Marlon Anderson capping it with a solo shot. All seven homers came between the fifth and seventh innings.

The following season, exactly one year and a day later, the Phillies surrendered nine home runs to the Cincinnati Reds—a National League single-game record that still stands.

2003—In its first regular season game at sparkling new Lincoln Financial Field, the Eagles looked to exact revenge on the Tampa Bay Buccaneers—the team that delivered one of the most painful defeats in team history the season prior in the NFC Championship game, the last at The Vet. Apparently not content with just *ending* a Birds' season on a somber note, the Bucs, by way of a 17-0 rout, made their menacing mark on the infancy of a 2003 season that would see the Birds rebound to 12-4 overall.

COLOR COMMENTARY

Rocky Balboa was there, as the Eagles opened up the Linc. Talk about too much hype, all style, and no substance—this was the game for all three.

The Birds get shut out 17-0 to Tampa Bay as the Philly faithful get introduced to the world of antiseptic architecture, all in the name of luxury boxes and Builder Seats Licenses.

The Eagles will eventually win an NFC game here in 2004, but The Linc is no Veterans Stadium. It may have more bathrooms and more choices for concessions, but still to this day, lacks the energy and the fire the Vet possessed. I guess we just can't stand in the way of change.

9th

1997—Richie "Whitey" Ashburn, Phillies Hall of Fame centerfielder and broadcaster, died of a heart attack on this date in New York after calling a game at Shea Stadium. After 15 years on the diamond (12 with Philadelphia), and 34 years in the Phils broadcast booth, Whitey had just begun to think about retirement at the time of his passing. Having already received his long-overdue enshrinement into the National Baseball Hall of Fame in 1995, with little left to accomplish, Ashburn, according to his mother, had planned on calling it a career after the '97 season.

The Phillies' radio broadcast booth at Citizens Bank Park is named The Richie "Whitey" Ashburn Broadcast Booth in his honor.

2015—The Temple Owls football program enjoyed its first win over Penn State in 74 years, besting the Nittany Lions 27-10, in front of a sold out Lincoln Financial Field crowd.

It was one of the best wins in the school's 117 seasons, as Temple was mired in an astonishingly-dismal 39-game winless streak against PSU, with just a single tie to hang its hat on since 1941 (0-38-1). The Owls' previous win over the Nittany Lions came less than two months before the attack on Pearl Harbor.

Temple was ranked as high as No. 22 in the AP Top 25 in 2015—a feat, in itself, entirely unthinkable just a decade ago, when the Big East dropped the school and Temple officials had considered pulling the program. By their ninth game of 2015, the Owls had doubled the team's win total in the four seasons from 2003-06, combined.

10th

1980—Making his first Major League start, Phils rookie Marty Bystrom pitched a clutch five-hit complete game shutout over the Mets (5-0), to fuel a late-season pennant run. Bystrom, remarkably, won *all five* of his regular season starts to close out the season, going into the playoffs with a 5-0 record and 1.50 ERA. Each of those five wins was crucial, as the Phils won the East that year by just a single game over the runner-up Montreal Expos.

Unfortunately, Bystrom's early returns never carried over to a long and prosperous Major League career. His five wins at the tail-end of the '80 regular season, though, helped get the nearly-100-year-old franchise its first championship. In the end, that's enough to carry an everlasting legacy.

11th

We could tell you that in 2004, the Phillies used 10 pitchers in a 13-inning, 11-9 win over the New York Mets. We could also inform you about an 18-year-old kid named Freddy Van Dusen, who debuted for the Phillies in 1955 as a pinch hitter. He was hit by a pitch in his first and only plate appearance in the majors. Tough break, kid.

But we all know why this day is so very important, and will be forever.

9/11/01 God Bless America. Never Forget.

12th

1958—In a 19-2 loss to the San Francisco Giants, the Phillies fielded their first black pitcher in franchise history, right-handed reliver Hank Mason, who surrendered six runs in five innings of work.

Though Hank "Pistol" Mason never quite caught on in the Major Leagues (just 10 2/3 career innings pitched), his 95-mph heater led him to successful stints in the Negro Leagues and minor league ball.

1999—Andy Reid's coaching debut for the Philadelphia Eagles represented a turning point for the franchise—but change was slow to come, as the Eagles, coming off a 3-13 season, blew a 21-point lead in a 25-24 loss to the Cardinals.

13th

1924—For its fifth straight victory in the 19th annual International Lawn Tennis Challenge (known today as the Davis Cup), the United States defeated Australia (5-0) at the Germantown Cricket Club, the event's first-ever stop in Philadelphia.

14th

2006—Keith Primeau announced his retirement from the Flyers and the NHL on this date, after nearly a year-long battle with post-concussion maladies. Primeau, one of the Flyers' all-time great team captains, according to then-GM Bob Clarke, was a fan-favorite in his workmanlike six seasons for the Orange & Black.

(*AP Photo*)

"I'm sorry I couldn't overcome this injury and dragged this out as long as I did," Primeau said in his farewell address. "I did it all with the best of intentions and with the thought of returning home and playing in front of 20,000 screaming fans."

15th

1987—Mike Schmidt hit his 30th home run of the season, in a 4-3 loss to the St. Louis Cardinals. With the blast, Schmidt set a new Phillies record for 30-homer seasons, with 13 over the course of his illustrious 18-year career. The record still stands, and it stands very strong.

The combined 30-home run seasons of Phillies greats Ryan Howard, Chase Utley, Jayson Werth, and Bobby Abreu still come up just one short of the total Schmidt accrued all on his own.

1997—With the final seconds fleeting and down 21-20 to the Dallas Cowboys on *Monday Night Football*, Eagles quarterback Ty Detmer completed a 46-yard pass to Freddie Solomon inside the Dallas five-yard line. Needing just a chip-shot field goal to put the game away, Eagles holder Tommy Hutton fumbled the snap, and with it, the game. The heartbreaking loss set the tone for the team's abysmal 6-9-1 final standing.

16th

1960—Well, this is embarrassing. On this date, the Phillies were no-hit for the second time on the season, less than a month after the first—by the same team.

Milwaukee Braves' hurler Lew Burdette threw the first no-no in a 1-0 blanking of the Phils on August 18th, while a 39-year old Warren Spahn, the oldest player at the time to accomplish the feat (he'd break his own record a year later), got one of his own on this date. It was the shortest time span between no-hitters involving the same two teams in Major League history.

And while the Phillies don't even crack the top 5 in shortest time span between getting no-hit (by any team), that doesn't mean a Philly team is off the hook—The Philadelphia A's were no-hit twice over a four-day period in 1923 (by the New York Yankees on September 4th and the Boston Red Sox on September 7th).

17th

1989—Five touchdown passes and a team-record 447 passing yards helped Randall Cunningham and the Eagles eke out a 42-37 win over the Washington Redskins at RFK Stadium. Cunningham's passing yards surpassed the previous record, which had stood for 35 years (437 by Bobby Thomason, 1953).

The record is now held by Donovan McNabb, who threw for 464 on December 5th, 2004, against the Packers.

18th

1971—Rick Wise wasn't just a one-trick-pony during his brief stint in Philadelphia (see June 23rd). Aside from his no-hitter/two-home-run day, Wise had another historical day on the mound (and at the plate) on this date, retiring 32 straight batters in a complete game, 12-inning victory (4-3) over the Chicago Cubs.

After surrendering three runs to the Cubbies by the second inning, Wise tossed 10 2/3 perfect innings from then on, giving up just a harmless single to Ron Santo in the 12th. As the Phils offense couldn't muster anything on their end either, Wise took it upon himself, hitting a walk-off single in the bottom of the 12th with two outs and the bases loaded.

Wise's run of 32 consecutive outs is thirteen shy of the current Major League record (45, Mark Buehrle, 2009).

19th

1999—Not to be confused with his first start (see November 14th), Eagles quarterback Donovan McNabb made his first *appearance* in a game on this date, relieving starter Doug Pederson in the second half of a dreary 19-5 loss to the Tampa Bay Buccaneers.

The franchise leader in pass completions (2,801), passing yards (32,873), and passing touchdowns (216), McNabb would begin his career with a whimper. He was just 4-for-11 in his Birds debut, for a scant 26 yards.

2013—On the 14th anniversary of McNabb's debut, the Eagles retired the quarterback's No. 5 jersey at halftime of an eventual 26-16 loss to the Kansas City Chiefs.

The all-time winningest quarterback in franchise history (92-49-1), while sometimes criticized for his hot and cold relationship with the fans and the city of Philadelphia, McNabb reassured the sell-out crowd at Lincoln Financial Field:

"I stand here to let you know I truly love and respect everything you've given me for 10 years. I stand here, and from the bottom of my heart, to let you know I truly appreciate everything you've done for me. Words cannot say how much I truly love you. Those 10 banners up there, six of them, we are responsible for. And I want you to understand that. So if you don't feel this energy that's going down right now, No. 5 will always love you. The City of Brotherly Love, thank you."

20th

1992—Phillies second baseman Mickey Morandini turned the franchise's first unassisted triple play, in a 3-2 loss to the Pirates. Catching Jeff King's liner, Morandini stepped on second base (forcing out Andy Van Slyke) and tagged Barry Bonds to complete just the ninth unassisted triple play in league history.

Eric Bruntlett's in 2008 was the second for the Phils (15th total) and the second in Major League history to end a ballgame.

2001—During the second intermission of a preseason hockey game between the Flyers and New York Rangers, the First Union Center Jumbotron showed President George W. Bush's State of the Union address, nine days following the 9/11 attacks in New York.

Morandini earned his only career All-Star appearance for the Phils in 1995. (*Dealphungo*)

At the speech's conclusion, both Flyers and Rangers players shook hands and agreed to end the game prematurely, with just two periods played in a 2-2 tie.

21st

1883—John Coleman lost his 48th game—that's not a typo—of the season for the Quakers/Phillies in a 9-3 loss to Detroit in Philadelphia's inaugural season.

In an era when starters finished what they started, and staffs consisted of far less specialty hurlers than we see in today's game, Coleman's Major League records that season for losses (48), runs allowed (510), and hits allowed (772) will never be broken. He had the unfortunate distinction of playing for the wrong team in the wrong era.

COLOR COMMENTARY

So much for the importance of "innings eaters." Coleman was actually Philadelphia's best starter that first season. Unfortunately, he was the best starter on one of the worst professional baseball teams ever put together.

There is some positive spin to Coleman's brutal season—with a 12-48 record, he accounted for 71% of the team's victories that season (17-81 overall).

Coleman, seen here with Pittsburgh in 1887, blossomed into the team's best hitter (*Library of Congress*)

22nd

1949—The Eagles played their first game under the new ownership group, "The Happy Hundred," an eventual 7-0 win over the New York Bulldogs.

Former owner Alexis Thompson sold the team to 100 buyers, each purchasing a single share priced at $3,000.

Shown here in his prime in 1921, Dempsey is ranked #10 on *The Ring Magazine*'s list of all-time heavyweights (*Library of Congress*)

Coming off the team's first championship in '48, there was no layover in '49 under the new leadership, as the Eagles finished at 12-1, repeating as NFL champs.

2008—Conventional wisdom says that pitching wins championships in Major League Baseball, but the Phillies' pitching staff was not their greatest asset in 2008. Sure, ace Cole Hamels won the World Series MVP, pitching lights-out baseball in the postseason, but it was Philadelphia's bats that got them to the big stage.

The Phillies had a franchise-best 18-game home run streak, from September 3-22, which helped the Phillies wrestle another NL East title away in the season's final days. By the start of the streak, the Phils were 3 games back in the division. By the end, they were 2.5 up, and the hottest team in baseball.

23rd

Two bouts occurred on this date that are interchangeable, often leading the debate on the most important fights in city history.

1926—The highlight event of the new Sesquicentennial/Municipal/JFK Stadium saw Gene Tunney defeat Jack Dempsey for the heavyweight title. Tunney won by unanimous decision, but the fight set off a rivalry between the two boxing legends that captured the nation.

In their two-bout series, both won by Tunney, the duo set gate receipt records, spurned Al Capone (a big Dempsey fan, and influential bettor/fixer) by moving the first fight outside of the organized crime leader's Chicago fortress, and created national controversy over the second fight's winner (because of a supposed "long" 10-second knockdown count by the referee on Tunney).

The first bout in Philadelphia was in front of a record 120,557 rain-soaked fans at Municipal.

1952—In another battle of titans, also at Municipal Stadium in Philadelphia, Rocky Marciano furthered his career undefeated record and captured the heavyweight title with a 13th-round knockout of Jersey Joe Walcott.

The fight, by today's standards, might not have turned out so well for Marciano. Having been knocked down in the first round, the tough-as-nails (Balboa-esque, even) Marciano was down on the cards until the 13th-round knockout—a time when modern 12-round title fights would be over.

The victory began a four-year span of successful title defenses (including a first-round knockout of Walcott in the rematch) as Marciano retired with the championship intact in '56.

1983—Steve Carlton won his 300th game, a 6-2 victory over the St. Louis Cardinals, the team that contentiously traded the four-time Cy Young winner to Philadelphia in 1972.

Lefty, despite playing for six different teams during his career, is the Phils' all-time leader in wins (241).

24th

1950—Russ Craft, a member of the 1948/49 Eagles championship teams, earned an individual honor, collecting an NFL-record four interceptions in a single game, in a 45-7 romp of the Chicago Cardinals. Nineteen other players currently share the record.

25th

1932—Despite an 0-for-8 day at the plate, Phils Hall of Famer Chuck Klein was still able to make history.

His hitless doubleheader, on the last day of the season, notwithstanding, Klein finished the season with 38 home runs and 20 stolen bases, to lead the league in both categories. And Klein's accomplishment has yet to be duplicated.

While he was the third player in history to lead the league in both categories (Jimmy Sheckard and Ty Cobb were the others), Klein is credited as the only player in the "Live-Ball Era" (post-1920) to do it.

2007—Building on an MVP 2007 season, Jimmy Rollins joined Bobby Abreu (2001) as the only member of the Phillies to steal 30 bases and slug 30 home runs in the same season.

While the 30/30 club is clearly less exclusive today than it was pre-1990 (just 17 of the current 60-such seasons occurred before 1990), Rollins' 30 homer/41 stolen base season was still just the 50th 30/30 in Major League history. But he didn't stop there.

With a triple in his last at-bat, Rollins finished the season with 38 doubles, 20 triples, 30 home runs, and 41 stolen bases, becoming just the *fourth* player ever to go 20/20/20/20.

26th

1976—Sweeping the doubleheader series with the Montreal Expos (4-1, 2-1), the Phillies clinched the first National League East title in franchise history.

Major League Baseball's four-division format was instituted in 1969, and abandoned in 1994 in favor of the current six-division alignment. In that 25-year span, Pennsylvania accounted for 15 NL East titles in all (Pittsburgh, 9; Philadelphia, 6).

27th

1924—A Philadelphia team played its first game in the National Football League—and it wasn't the Eagles.

Philly's own Frankford Yellow Jackets defeated the Rochester Jeffersons, 21-0, en route to an 11-2-1 record that should not exactly be attributed to beginner's luck.

The early days of the NFL were structured similarly to the college football system. Teams were free to schedule their own games, particularly against non-NFL clubs, with an inexact cap on league competition. So, before the team was accepted into the NFL, it was a highly successful independent club and frequent scrimmage-mate of league teams (including a competitive 3-0 loss to the reigning NFL champion Canton Bulldogs in 1923).

The Yellow Jackets certainly hit the ground running in 1924, and during their eight-season NFL run, no team scheduled more league games.

Unfortunately for the Yellow Jackets, their relentless avidity worked against them in two ways—more games meant a higher probability for injuries and also more opportunities for notches in the loss column. Because the league's standings were based purely on winning percentage, more games simply invited amplified risk. For one season, though, that risk was rewarded.

By the end of the 1926 season, the Yellow Jackets stood at 14-1-2, claiming the league crown. And while they were not long for the NFL (due primarily to financial reasons they disbanded after the 1931 season), the league record had a half-century-long staying power, bested by the 15-1 San Francisco 49ers in 1984.

28th

1958—Acquired via an offseason trade, Eagles quarterback Norm Van Brocklin played his first game for the Birds, passing for just a shade over 100 yards and rushing for one TD in a 14-24 loss to the Washington Redskins.

Van Brocklin, a six-time Pro Bowler with the LA Rams, eventually got the offense going in Philadelphia, quarterbacking the team to a 10-2 record in 1960 and winning the NFL Championship—Philly's last NFL title.

Van Brocklin was inducted into the Pro Football Hall of Fame in 1971.

29th

1986—For the first time in Major League history, two rookie brothers pitched against each other, as Greg Maddux and the Chicago Cubs defeated Mike Maddux and the Phillies, 8-3.

COLOR COMMENTARY

Just add Mike Maddux to the list: Vince DiMaggio, Frank Torre, Mark Leiter, Jeremy Giambi, etc. The Phillies always got the "wrong" brother.

It was just one of 355 career victories for the younger brother, Greg, who stymied Phils hitters for over a decade with the NL East Atlanta Braves.

2002—In a 35-17 win over the Houston Texans, Eagles Pro Bowl safety Brian Dawkins became the first player in NFL history to record a sack, interception, forced fumble, and touchdown in the same game.

One of the most popular and talented Eagles of all time, Dawkins was a six-time All-Pro.

COLOR COMMENTARY

I have been going to Eagles home games for 25 years, and this may have been the single, greatest individual performance I had ever seen from a player wearing Philadelphia green.

And the best part about it was that it was Brian Dawkins, who was well on his way to being one of the most beloved Eagles of all time. Dawkins epitomized what it meant to be a Philadelphia athlete, and played the game with such desire and emotion.

He finished his time with the Eagles having started 182 of 183 games, completed 898 tackles, tallied 34 interceptions, collected 32 forced fumbles, and recorded 21 sacks. He is an Eagle Hall of Famer whose bust will reside in Canton someday soon.

30th

Dawkins' TD was the only one of his illustrious 13-year NFL career. (*Philadelphia Eagles*)

1885—Bobby Mathews of the Philadelphia Athletics (then of the American Association) became the first pitcher in professional baseball history to strike out *four* batters in a single inning.

Technically, there's an infinite amount of possible strikeouts that can be accumulated in any given inning. If a catcher does not field a swinging strike three cleanly, the batter has the opportunity to reach base safely, unless thrown out at first. If the runner beats the throw in such a scenario, the out is nixed, but the *strikeout* remains.

To add to Mathews' feat, he is the only person to ever accomplish this during the World Series.

1964—The Phold.

On this date in '64, the Phillies dropped their 10th straight game, an 8-5 loss to the St. Louis Cardinals, to set up the most colossal collapse in Major League history.

The Phils would win the following two games, the last of the season, but it wasn't enough, as the Cards held on to take the pennant by a game over Philadelphia. The first team in history to blow a six-and-a-half-game lead with 12 to play, the Phillies—of all teams, the perennially woeful Phillies—had found a new way to break Philadelphia fans' bleeding baseball hearts.

Philadelphia author Joe Queenan put the feeling to words in 1996:

This was the pivotal event in my life. Nothing good that has ever happened to me since then can make up for the disappointment of that ruined season, and nothing bad that has happened since then can even vaguely compare with the emotional devastation wrought by that monstrous collapse.

The "phantom" World Series ticket of 1964

2007—Not only had the Phillies failed to win a World Series since 1980, but also they hadn't even sniffed the postseason in 14 years, before they finally clinched the NL East, via a 6-1 win over the Washington Nationals on the final day of the season in 2007.

The game was doubly sweet, as the Phils win, coupled with a Mets loss, knocked New York from playoff contention, and rid the Phils of a pesky distinction that had stuck with them since 1964. Major League Baseball had a new goat to pick on.

The Phils' '64 collapse (celebrating its anniversary) was suddenly a fading memory, as the Mets became the first Major League team to blow a seven-game lead with 17 games remaining. The young Phillies squad was establishing the building blocks of a world championship squad, and the Mets were going down in flames—the stars were aligning in Philadelphia.

~AND~

2007 (After the Phillies clinched)—Tra Thomas' injury would help dubiously define the career of backup left tackle Winston Justice, as the Eagles squared off against the division foe New York Giants on *Sunday Night Football*. By the final whistle, Justice had allowed six sacks, all to Giants defensive end Osi Umenyiora. In the 16-3 win, the Giants tied a league record, sacking quarterback Donovan McNabb 12 times.

COLOR COMMENTARY

Not unlike the Eagles' NFC Championship breakthrough in 2004–05, the unparalleled joy was in, simply, "just getting there." Sure, all the Phillies accomplished was a postseason berth with no promises of a parade down Broad Street, but, with apologies to all those disenchanted Atlanta Braves fans, that's still a pretty big deal.

Maybe it's no biggie for teams like the Patriots and Steelers to make the Super Bowl, or the Yankees and Braves to glide into the postseason with relative ease. But in Philadelphia, these things never come cheap. When Brett Myers struck out Wily Mo Peña to clinch the postseason on this day, I had only ever seen such a thing one other time in my life. It was something new and exciting. For me, and a whole generation, "just getting there" was enough.

1st

1980—Saving his best for last, Steve Carlton pitched, arguably, his best game of the season, a complete-game, two-hit, shutout victory over the Chicago Cubs, 5-0.

In the game, Carlton also passed the 300-inning plateau (304 in all), becoming the last (likely ever) pitcher to pitch 300 frames in a single season.

2006—With a single in a 3-2 Phillies loss to the Florida Marlins, Ryan Howard finished his MVP season with the highest amount of total bases (383) for Philadelphia since Chuck Klein had 420 playing in baseball's original "bandbox" Baker Bowl.

Howard also finished with the third-highest runs-created total that season (169), which is a stat that estimates a player's contributions to a team's total scoring output. It was the highest mark since Klein in 1930 (193).

2nd

1916—Ace Grover Cleveland Alexander notched his 33rd win of the season (33-12 overall), establishing a new Phillies single-season record that still stands.

Nineteen-sixteen was the second of three straight seasons in which Alexander won pitching's Triple Crown, leading the National League in wins, ERA, and strikeouts. The Phils' single-season (1.22, 1915) and career (2.18; minimum 1,000 IP) ERA leader was named after the nation's 22nd president, Grover Cleveland. Ironically, former president Ronald Reagan would later play the role of Alexander in the 1952 film *The Winning Team*.

1943—The *Steagles* played their first game on this date, a 17-0 victory over the Brooklyn Dodgers.

With rosters helplessly depleted due to the wartime draft, the Eagles and Pittsburgh Steelers squads were forced to merge to keep the teams—and league—afloat.

Consisting of only draft deferments, the Steagles (officially, the NFL recognizes the team as Phil-Pitt/Eagles-Steelers) roster consisted mostly of draft rejects and older vets. Because of this, not only was the team ill-fit to field a talented squad, but also the players were required by law to hold full-time jobs to support the war effort, as professional football was, at the time, considered extracurricular.

The Steagles lasted just one season, posting a 5-4-1 record (the Eagles' first winning season in the NFL) before disbanding. With the Army's declaration that men over 26 would no longer be drafted, the NFL resumed healthy operation in 1944, and both the Eagles and Steelers were able to field separate teams—sort of.

With the expansion Boston Yanks coming in, the league consisted of 11 teams, which posed major scheduling problems. The Steelers, perhaps unwilling to coexist with the rival Eagles for one more season, merged with the Chicago Cardinals in '44 instead. The Card-Pitt team, mockingly nicknamed the *Carpets,* got walked over by every opponent en route to a winless, 0-10 season—the first of five winless teams in NFL history.

Fun Fact: The Steagles held the Dodgers to minus-33 rushing yards, the third-lowest single game rushing total in league history.

1965—The Phillies and New York Mets played 18 consecutive scoreless innings, and that's exactly how the game would end—in a scoreless tie. Both teams' starting pitchers—Christ

Short for the Phillies and Rob Gardner for the Mets—pitched 15 innings apiece before giving it up to the bullpen. Short, pitching in his final start of the season, was particularly dazzling, striking out 18, setting a new team record.

In his final two starts of the season, Short gave up just two earned runs over a 24-inning span, dropping his season ERA from 3.00 to 2.82, putting him in the top ten in league ERA for 1965.

3rd

1972—Completing one of the most dominating seasons ever pitched in Major League history, Steve Carlton collected his league-leading 27th win in a complete-game 11-1 Phillies victory over the Chicago Cubs.

He also finished the year tops in ERA (1.97) and strikeouts (310), to round out the pitching triple crown, and from June 7th to August 17th, Lefty was 15-0. But the most remarkable fact regarding Carlton's 27-win gem is that it was accomplished on a 59-win Phillies team. He had single handedly accounted for almost half of the team's wins.

Said Hall of Fame slugger Willie Stargell on facing Carlton:

"Hitting him is like trying to drink coffee with a fork."

4th

1980—Before the championship parade, World Series, and NLCS, the Phils eked out a victory against the Expos on this date, the second-to-last day of the regular season, to clinch the National League East.

Tied at four in the 11th inning, Mike Schmidt hit a two-run home run to give the Phils a 6-4 lead. Tug McGraw closed it out in the bottom half, and the Phillies were NL East champions.

Schmidt's 48 home run total led the league and was a franchise record.

2015—Phillies closer Ken Giles pitched a perfect ninth inning, finishing off the season with a 7-2 win over the Miami Marlins. Giles finished the season with a 1.80 ERA, putting his career mark at 1.56—which gave him, for now, the lowest career ERA in baseball history (minimum 100 innings pitched).

5th

1916—The legendary Billy Maharg made his one and only plate appearance for the Phillies. It's enough to make the diminutive 5-foot-4 infielder the shortest player in team history, but Maharg's legend is much taller.

The former Philadelphia boxer made a name for himself behind the scenes in Major League Baseball, as one of the primary middle men (and whistle blowers) of the 1919 Black Sox scandal.

Maharg, rumored to have concocted his last name from "Graham" spelled backwards, first contacted Philly newspapers in 1920 about the infamous 1919 World Series fix. His reasons for coming clean are unclear, but it is believed that Maharg was cheated by his cohorts, most notably among them infamous gangster Arnold Rothstein.

He was portrayed by 6-foot actor Richard Edson in the film *Eight Men Out*.

1929—Phillies outfielder Lefty O'Doul smacked two hits in a 12-3 loss to the New York Giants, establishing a new single-season hits record for both the Phillies and the National League (254). The two base knocks came during the final game of the season, and the end of a season-best 15-game hitting streak.

O'Doul, though not a household name in Philadelphia, was a tremendously important player. He had Hall of Fame talent, but didn't play much until he reached his 30s. His batting average during his first five full seasons, was .365.

He is credited with helping grow the popularity of baseball in Japan, and was one of the most influential figures on the San Francisco baseball scene, taking a successful turn managing the minor league Seals of the Bay Area, before opening a popular restaurant in San Fran that still bears his name.

Roy Hobbs' character in *The Natural* is said to be partially based on Lefty.

1988—The Eagles traded their first-round pick to the Colts for offensive guard Ron Solt. A Pro Bowler the season prior, Solt played two quarters for the Eagles before missing the rest of the season with a knee injury. Who did the Colts get with Philly's first-round pick? Five-time Pro Bowler Andre Rison. Solt was out of the league after four seasons with the team.

6th

1923—The Phillies have turned more than their fair share of unassisted triple plays, but on this date, they were on the wrong end of the first unassisted triple play in National League history. The Boston Braves' Ernie Padgett turned the trick in the last game of the regular season.

Carlos "Chooch" Ruiz embracing his
unhittable battery mate Roy Halladay.
(see page 249). *(AP Photo/Matt
Rourke)*

2010—Roy Halladay wasn't perfect on this date, but almost. In his first postseason appearance, Roy Halladay tossed the second playoff no-hitter in baseball history, blanking the Reds 4-0 in the opening round of the NLDS.

It was the first postseason no-hitter in the playoffs since Don Larsen's perfecto in '56, and the first time a pitcher tossed two no-no's in the same season since Nolan Ryan turned the trick in '73.

COLOR COMMENTARY

Growing up, I had heard of Don Larsen's perfect game, but never really thought it was possible to replicate. And then came Doc. His performance reminded me that, on any given day, baseball history can be made, and connections to past legends and historic accomplishments can fuse in an instant.

7th

1969—The Phillies signed off on perhaps the most influential trade in baseball history.

When the Phillies agreed to send Cookie Rojas, Dick Allen, and Jerry Johnson to the St. Louis Cardinals for Tim McCarver, Byron Browne, Joe Hoerner, and Curt Flood, they had no idea that the transaction would become a Supreme Court case.

COLOR COMMENTARY

Although Flood was a very good .293 career hitter with St. Louis, it wasn't a J. D. Drew–esque debacle for Philadelphia. As compensation, the Phils received Willie Montanez, a decent player in his own right and 14-year veteran of Major League Baseball.

There's much dispute over why Flood wanted out of the trade to Philadelphia. The Phillies were among the worst teams in baseball, having lost 99 games in '69, with a less than stellar track record dating nearly acentury back. So while that alone could well have been it, there were other factors.

For one, the Phillies were the last National League squad to break their team's color barrier—Richie Ashburn once spoke of Roy Campanella's desire to play for Philadelphia and the Phillies' ideology that prevented the Hall of Fame backstop from realizing his dream. Over the years, Flood gave reasons for his decision, some specific and targeted, and others general and contradictory.

Of the most poignant, years later, he referenced the Kennedys and Martin Luther King, Jr. as inspirations for his move:

"[T]o think that merely because I was a professional baseball player, I could ignore what was going on outside the walls of Busch Stadium was truly hypocrisy and now I found that all of those rights that these great Americans were dying for, I didn't have in my own profession."

The truth is probably an amalgam of everything—understandable, given his sudden upheaval from St. Louis. Given other options, I wouldn't want to play for the '60s-era Phillies either, for its win-loss record alone. But it's important to not forget Flood's place in sports history.

His efforts pale in comparison, and came a couple decades after Jackie Robinson's courageous first steps in Dodger Blue, but Flood shouldn't be overlooked for his efforts in '69 and thereafter. As fans, we may scoff at giant salaries too often attributed to minimal effort, and skyrocketing ticket prices that rarely drive up ticks in the win column, but Flood was paramount in at least creating the (relatively) free market system we see today. He balanced the power between players and management, and although it's becoming increasingly more difficult to relate to these millionaire athletes, the fight for fairness and freedom in the workplace is always a noble one.

Flood, contesting Major League Baseball's reserve clause, which essentially tied a player to a specific team for life, refused to report to Philadelphia, and sat out the entire 1970 season. Likening the ownership and swapping of Major League players to slavery, Flood's case reached the US Supreme Court, which in a 5-3 ruling, upheld baseball's rule—briefly.

Fans were siding heavily with the players on the issue during the long, drawn-out battle, and the tide of change was inevitable. In 1975, an independent arbitrator granted players Andy Messersmith and Dave McNally "free agent" status and ushered in the free market system employed by Major League Baseball today.

Black Friday, 1977—Tied at a game apiece in the best-of-five NLCS, the Phillies led the Dodgers in Game 3, 5-3 in the top of the ninth, with two outs and the bases empty. A bunt single, and fielding blunders by Greg Luzinski and Ted Sizemore—on the same play—landed the Phils in a precarious situation, holding onto a 5-4 lead, with a runner on third base, and Davey Lopes at the plate for LA.

What followed was reminiscent of the infamous "pebble play" that highlighted Game 7 of the 1924 World Series between the New York Giants and Washington Senators, perhaps the greatest game ever played. In the 12th inning, a routine ground ball to third reportedly hit a pebble and careened into left field, allowing the winning run to score for the Senators.

In the Phillies' case, the routine ground ball to third hit a seam in the Veterans Stadium turf, bouncing off of Mike Schmidt to Larry Bowa, who completed a bare-handed gem to first, seemingly just ahead of a chugging Lopes—only First Base Umpire Bruce Froemming didn't see it that way. Froemming called Lopes safe, plating the tying run. Lopes eventually scored the game-winner, on a single by Bill Russell, snatching a critical 2-1 series lead and a World Series berth the following day.

It was Philadelphia's own personal *Shock* Heard 'Round the World—coined "Black Friday" by the press, it was more of the same for the anemic franchise, and perhaps the first in a long line of slanderous black marks on Vet Stadium's infamous playing surface.

8th

1887—The Phillies/Quakers, on the final day of the season, won their 16th straight game, a team record that still stands after all these years.

The streak actually spanned 17 games (one was a tie), as Major League Baseball does not recognize tie games as a disruption of winning streaks.

"The Babe," looking not-quite-right without his Yankee pinstripes
(*Library of Congress*)

1915—Before 1980, not only had the Phillies never won a World Series title, but also the team had only one World Series victory under its belt—on this date.

Grover Cleveland Alexander got the win (3-1) for the Phils in Game 1 over the Boston Red Sox. It was the only game decided by more than one run, as Boston eked out the next four by a single run apiece, behind the game's top starting rotation. Perhaps just to rub it in, the Sox took home the title with their best pitcher (yes, *pitcher*), Babe Ruth, never toeing the rubber.

9th

1983—Bill Barber became the first Flyer to score his 400th career NHL goal, the 19th player in league history to reach the career milestone. The Flyers won the game, 7-1, over the Pittsburgh Penguins.

Barber, a career Flyer, still holds the team record for goals, with 420 in his 13 seasons in the NHL.

10th

1993—A season on the threshold of brilliance had been (literally) broken in an instant. In a Week 5 game against the Chicago Bears, starting quarterback Randall Cunningham suffered a broken leg—ending his season and stifling the team's high hopes at once. Starting off 4-0, Cunningham could no longer fly, and the team's wings had effectively been clipped. The Eagles finished 8-8, hampered by the second season-ending injury to Cunningham in three years.

11th

1959—During a game at Franklin Field between the Eagles and Pittsburgh Steelers, league commissioner and founder of the Birds, Bert Bell, died of a heart attack while watching the final minutes on the sidelines.

A titan amongst Philadelphians in sports history, the UPenn graduate brought the NFL back to Philadelphia in 1933 after the Frankford Yellow Jackets folded two years prior.

As commissioner, Bell was instrumental in developing the league's anti-gambling policies and for nurturing the game's growth, despite foolishly declaring in 1951, "You can't give the fans a game for free on TV and also expect them to go to the ballpark." Nevertheless, the compromise of gate sales and TV growth would eventually lead to the TV blackout rules we see today, when only sell-outs hit the airwaves.

1979—In his first NHL game, touted rookie forward (drafted 14th overall) Brian Propp scored his first career goal, part of a 5-2 Flyers win over the New York Islanders. Propp was an immediate success in the league, scoring 34 goals his rookie season, en route to a tremendous 425-goal career (369 with Philadelphia). His trademark "guffaw!" celebrations, and prolific offensive consistency—Propp is second to only Bill Barber in Flyers career goals—made the Saskatchewan native a fan favorite in Philadelphia.

12th

2003—Eagles head coach Andy Reid called for an opening onside kick against the Dallas Cowboys—a surprise play that had proved successful three seasons prior. Only this time around, Randal Williams of the Cowboys collected the kick and scored three seconds into regulation—the fastest score in NFL history.

It was costly—the Eagles lost the game, 23-21.

13th

1915—On their first attempt, the Phillies lost the World Series to the Boston Red Sox, with a 5-4 Game 5 loss.

Despite having the league's lowest ERA (2.17) and leading the National League in home runs (58—the same amount Ryan Howard hit *by himself* in 2006), the Phils couldn't quite put it all together against the American League's best. Combined, both teams scored a total of just 13 runs through the first four games of the best-of-seven series.

All but one of the games was decided by just a single run (Game 1, which Phillies won, 3-1, was the exception).

1993—The high point of the Phillies' worst-to-first turnaround season came on this day. Comprised of a lovable group of mostly castoffs and zany characters, they capped

The 1915 NL Champion Phillies (*Bain News Service*)

their 97-win season with an unlikely Game 6 NLCS-clinching win over the Atlanta Braves, 6-3.

Curt Schilling won the NLCS MVP award with a 1.69 ERA in two starts, leading the Phils to just their fifth World Series appearance in over 100 years.

14th

1979—With a 4-3 win over the Toronto Maple Leafs in the third game of the season, the Flyers began one of the most successful stretches in Philadelphia sports history. Over the next 34 games, the Flyers did not lose.

Putting together two consecutive *months* without a loss (November, December), Philadelphia racked up a 25-0-10 record, smashing the league's previous unbeaten record of 28 games (Montreal Canadiens, 1977–78). They finally dropped one on January 7th of 1980, but it didn't slow them down.

Through 60 games, the Flyers were a video game–like 41-4-15 (on *easy mode*), and they even started the playoffs with a six-game winning streak, before ultimately bowing out to the New York Islanders in the Cup Finals.

15th

1977—Ed Tepper and Earl Foreman created the Major Indoor Soccer League. The Philadelphia Fever was the first of six franchises to be developed by the league.

In 1982, Lakers owner Jerry Buss purchased the team and moved the new "Los Angeles Lazers" out west.

It wasn't until 1996 that indoor soccer returned to the city as the Philadelphia Kixx, who were two-time MISL champions (2002, 2007), before shutting down after the 2010 season.

Never fear, indoor soccer fan(s)... the expansion Reading Roar are just a short drive away.

16th

1963—The former Syracuse Nationals played their first game as the new Philadelphia 76ers, winning 117-115 over the Detroit Pistons.

Struggling financially, the small market of Syracuse could no longer afford an NBA team. Conversely, Philadelphia was a booming basketball market, but had no team to call their own. The match was natural and inevitable.

After a one-year hiatus following the Warriors' move to San Francisco, NBA basketball was back in Philly. The members of the "76ers," (or "Sixers" for short) immediately clicked—signing the game's best player tends to make that pretty easy.

In 1965, Wilt Chamberlain, the Warriors star and Philly high school legend, was brought back to Philadelphia, acquired in a trade with San Francisco. Two seasons after that, Wilt's squad won a league-record 68 regular season games, en route to an NBA Finals victory over the Warriors.

1983—The Phillies' team nickname was the "Wheeze Kids"—not quite as inspiring as "Murderers Row"—but it was appropriate and indicative of what the Phillies were and were not capable of, bowing out to the Orioles in the World Series' fifth and deciding game on this date in 1983. The Game 5 loss was the representation of the Phils' championship window decidedly closing, as the holdovers from 1980's championship team were lagging and any and all young reinforcements were drastically substandard.

1994—Trailing the Dallas Cowboys, 24-13, late after a fourth-quarter touchdown, Eagles head coach Rich Kotite opted for a two-point conversion. The attempt failed, and the Eagles lost by the same score, but the conversion itself made headlines, as seemingly no statistical advantage is gained by trying for, or even completing, the two-point play.

Kotite's explanation proved legendary. "I must have read my chart wrong," Kotite offered. "It must have gotten wet."

The piece of paper that told Kotite what to do . . . must have gotten wet. It was his last season as coach of the Eagles.

17th

1954—Eagles quarterback Adrian Burk set a team record and tied the NFL mark with seven touchdown passes in a single game, in a 49-21 rout of the Washington Redskins.

COLOR COMMENTARY

When the dust settled on Foles' historic seven-touchdown game in 2013 (greatest statistical performance for a quarterback ever, in my opinion), there was time and opportunity to study the very interesting life of Foles' seven-touchdown clubmate, Adrian Burk.

Hall of Fame sports writer Ray Didinger wrote a wonderful piece on Burk's big game, and life, for the Eagles' team website following Peyton Manning's own seven-TD game to open the 2013 season. Who knew it would come back around to an Eagle just a couple months later?

Burk was a successful lawyer in Texas following his playing career, and later became a back judge in the NFL, responsible for the call on one of the most infamous plays in sports history—the Pittsburgh Steelers' Immaculate Reception.

But what I found most interesting was Burk's work, with his wife, as a volunteer missionary, of which he told Didinger in a 1987 interview, was "the best decision we ever made. We don't live lavishly, but we've never lived better."

Contrary to his performance in this game, Burk was not a great NFL quarterback. He played for seven years in the NFL, six with Philadelphia, throwing 89 interceptions to his 61 touchdowns and completing just 46.3% of his passes.

Burk is one of just seven NFL quarterbacks (the Eagles' Nick Foles among them; see November 3rd) to throw seven TDs in a single game.

Had he sat out on October 17th, 1954, and not thrown a single TD, Burk would not have thrown more touchdowns than interceptions in any of his seven NFL seasons.

18th

1967—The Philadelphia Flyers won the franchise's first game, defeating the St. Louis Blues on the road, 2-1. Captain Lou Angotti and Ed Hoekstra scored for the team, as the Orange & Black beat Hall of Fame goaltender Glenn Hall, who was making his debut for the Blues. Hoekstra jammed home the score after a scramble in front of Hall with 7:20 remaining in the third period.

19th

1983—With his career on a clear decline, the Phillies released Pete Rose, 42, coming off a season in which he hit just .245. The leader of the Phils' 1980 championship team, Rose hustled his way through three more seasons, with stops in Montreal and Cincinnati before his abrupt departure due to a lifetime ban by Major League Baseball for gambling infractions (see February 4th).

20th

1976—If not for a transaction that occurred on this day between the New Jersey Nets and 76ers, pro basketball history in Philadelphia would have been a lot less exciting.

That season, the Nets joined the NBA after the merger with the defunct ABA and were immediately blindsided by the New York Knicks, who demanded the Nets pay $4.8 million for infringing on the Knicks' established NBA territory. Already bogged down by league entrance fees, the Nets were cash-strapped, holding just one viable asset that could clear their

COLOR COMMENTARY

Without the deal, New Jersey surely would have switched immediate fates with Philly. With Nate Archibald, the Nets would have paired a fearsome duo with Dr. J leading the charge. Most likely, it would have been the Nets winning 50 games with the top attendance and a shot at the title—not the Sixers.

Re-writing history, though, can be tricky. We can say with relative certainty what the fate of the two clubs would have been under both circumstances for that 1976 season alone, but from there, it gets complicated.

Would the Sixers have won the championship in '83 without Dr. J? Maybe not, but then maybe the Sixers are put in a position to draft Bernard King in '77 or Larry Bird in '78 and win multiple rings.

One thing is certain: the deal got us one of the most exciting, iconic players in pro basketball history.

And we have the Knicks to thank—however painful that is.

(Steve Lipofsky at basketballphoto.com)

path into the NBA: Julius Erving, who was due a raise that team owner Roy Boe couldn't afford.

New Jersey sold Dr. J to the 76ers for $3 million. It took care of the Nets' financial obligations, but came at the cost of the two-time ABA champion, and three-time MVP.

Dr. J was the face of the ABA, with his high-flying nature and tremendous scoring ability, and didn't take long to adjust to NBA competition. He headlined the Sixers to number one in attendance, winning 50 regular season games before bowing out to the Portland Trail Blazers in the NBA Finals.

Off the court, he was immediately one of the first great marketable NBA stars, and, for a while, he was the last great Philadelphia champion, winning the last pro sports championship for Philadelphia ('83) before a 25-year drought.

1977—With the hottest start in franchise history, the Flyers, through four games, had compiled a 4-0-0 record, scoring 31 goals while conceding just three goals against.

And while those numbers seem absurd enough, consider this—the Flyers defeated the Pittsburgh Penguins on this night by a score of 11-0.

It's the largest shutout win in Flyers history and tied for the largest margin of victory (the Fly Guys defeated the Vancouver Canucks 13-2 on October 18th, 1984), in a game that capped a remarkably one-sided Philly-Pittsburgh series in 1977.

21st

1980—65,000+ fans packed Veterans Stadium hoping to see the Phillies' first World Series Championship—an accomplishment almost a century in the making.

They would be rewarded, as Tug McGraw struck out the Kansas City Royals' Willie Wilson in Game 6 of the World Series, victoriously leaping in the air and forever into the hearts of Philadelphia sports fans.

The Phillies had finally broken through, and although they had amassed a sturdy reputation as one of sports' most consistently futile franchises, on this day in 1980, they were number one.

"Everybody said we couldn't win," Larry Bowa proclaimed. "No, the Phillies aren't good enough. They don't have the heart, they don't have the character. We have all of the above. Believe me."

Financial Fact: The Series had the highest television ratings to date, scoring an average Nielson rating of 32.8 per game.

2009—For the first time in the team's 127-year existence, the Phillies returned to a second consecutive World Series.

On this date in '09, the Phillies defeated the Los Angeles Dodgers in Game 5 of the NLCS, 10-4, for their second consecutive National League crown. It was déjà vu all over again for the Dodgers as well, who fell to the Phils in five games in 2008's NLCS.

Ryan Howard, series MVP, batted .333, leading the series in both runs scored (five, tied with Jimmy Rollins and Jayson Werth) and RBI (eight).

22nd

2006—With just under one minute remaining in regulation, the Eagles found themselves at midfield, down six points to the Tampa Bay Buccaneers in Week 7. A spectacular 52-yard touchdown play from Brian Westbrook put the Birds up by a point, with 33 seconds left on the clock.

Place kicker Matt Bryant and the pesky Bucs made the most of it, however, knocking a team-record 62-yard kick through the uprights for the win, with time expiring. Tampa Bay 23, Philadelphia 21.

COLOR COMMENTARY

Hard to believe, but I was in Tampa for both the October 22 events (2006 and 2008), spaced out between a couple of years.

As for the Eagles' game, there's really nothing more I can say other than that I was sitting in the opposite end-zone just seconds before Bryant nailed the game winner, and I turned to my buddy and predicted, "You know he's hitting this, right?"

It was just a feeling I had from watching the Bucs on that final drive, aided by Eagles Defensive End Jerome McDougle, who was penalized 15 yards for grabbing a facemask on a tackle before drawing another 15-yarder when he kicked the official's flag. Dope.

It was like 105 degrees in that stadium, and then we had to walk out with our tail between our legs after what we thought was a sure victory. A great comeback that was thwarted in the final seconds.

Let's fast forward to 2008, shall we (see below)? I like that story better.

I made the trip to Tampa, hanging out with my friend Dave, a Philly transplant. It was a first for me, seeing the Phils in the World Series on the road. Chase Utley's first-inning homer set the tone, as a throng of Phillies fans rejoiced in the victory.

A few quick memories were the dumb blue Mohawks and annoying cowbells the Rays fans were sporting. Seems they were enjoying their gimmicks, while the many Phillies fans were enjoying the victory.

And oh, I spent more on beer and food than I did on the tickets. I paid less than $100.00 for a seat just a few rows behind the first base dugout. A few nights later in Philly, I sold a pair for ten times that!

Tampa may have had our number with the Lightning Cup and the Bucs' win at The Vet, but Philly will always have 2008!

2008—Playing in their first World Series game in 15 years, the visiting Phillies took Game 1 from the Tampa Bay Rays, 3-2.

Cole Hamels, the Series MVP, pitched seven solid innings—surrendering just two runs as Ryan Madson and Brad Lidge closed it out. The crucial Game 1 victory on enemy turf helped set up the first major sports championship for the City of Brotherly Love in over 25 years (see October 27th/29th).

23rd

1993—The worst-to-first dream season had come to an end, with the Phils losing to the Toronto Blue Jays, 8-6, in Game 6 of the 1993 World Series.

A five-run inning in the seventh got the Phils on top, 6-5, but the biggest inning of all was the ninth, as was usually the case with Mitch Williams on the mound. Williams, enjoying a career year, was nicknamed "Wild Thing" for a reason. While his pitches in 1993 were often un-hittable, his erratic tendencies made them, at times, un-*swingable*.

COLOR COMMENTARY

The Phillies lost to the Blue Jays in the World Series. By definition, the 1993 squad was a loser. Yet, it's one of the city's most cherished teams.

Sure, the second-best Eagles squad in '80, the 76ers of '01, and to a lesser extent, the Flyers of '87, continue to draw pleasant memories and a certain fond nostalgic sentiment, but they don't get a pass like the '93 Phils.

And it's because of personality. Too often, a team will lay claim to its "blue-collar" roster, distinguishing the relatable characteristics between its millionaire ballplayers and hard-working 9-to-5 fan base—and it's usually bogus. The '93 Phillies, though, were the real deal.

Whether it was beer-bellied couch-potato "everyman" John Kruk; tough-as-nails scrapper Lenny Dykstra; philosophical mad professor, prankster Larry Anderson; young, reckless lefty Mitch "Wild Thing" Williams; or the wise old sage, with knees held together with spit and duct tape, Darren Daulton, fans related to the team like no other in Philadelphia sports history.

As fans, we don't focus as much on the season's shortcomings, because we care so much about the players involved. It was lightning in a bottle—a brief, yet perfect collaboration of talent and personality.

We could continue to dwell on Joe Carter's walk-off in Game 5, but that would spoil all the fun.

And while, obviously, Joe Carter's walk-off home run with two men aboard and one out was the biggest hit of the season, and among the greatest blasts in postseason history, Rickey Henderson's at-bat to lead off the inning made it all possible.

Before a single pitch was thrown, Henderson called for a timeout—clearly a tactic to unnerve Williams. When time was called, Wild Thing was already tucked into his pre-windup routine, and wouldn't look toward the plate again until midway through his delivery. When his eyes finally popped up from his cooky lefty reliever-mandatory throwing motion, catcher Darren Daulton, Henderson, and the umpire had cleared home plate. Williams, with a split second to react, held on to the ball while short-arming the continuation of his follow-through.

What followed was a four-pitch walk to put the most dangerous base runner in Major League history on board, with his team just a single run down. Regardless of whether or not Henderson's timeout messed with Willams' concentration, it was one of the most important, and forgotten, at-bats in World Series history.

24th

1959—Wilt Chamberlain played his first NBA game, for the Philadelphia Warriors, after spending a year with the Harlem Globetrotters.

Chamberlain was a territorial pick of the Warriors in the 1959 draft (abandoned in '66, teams were allowed to forfeit their first-round draft selection to obtain any eligible player within a 50-mile radius), which was highly disputed due to his three-year college career way out at the University of Kansas. But Chamberlain was a special case—as he has always been.

A Philadelphia high school legend at Overbrook High, the Big Dipper made national headlines even before he ever had a sniff of college ball, tying the 7'1" athletic freak to Philadelphia at an abnormally early age. If Kansas had a territorial affiliation with an NBA team, it would have been moot, but his heralded roots in Philly were the next-closest thing to a hometown right.

The start, a 118-109 win over the New York Knicks, began a record streak for Chamberlain of 1,045 games (his career total) without fouling out, later bested only by former Sixers great Moses Malone (1,212).

25th

1987—The growing legend of coach Buddy Ryan leapt into the stratosphere among Eagles fans everywhere when Ryan stuck it to the rival Cowboys. With the Eagles holding possession in the waning moments, leading Dallas 30-20 at Veterans Stadium, Ryan instructed quarterback Randall Cunningham to fake the kneel down and spike as Keith Byars slashed into the end zone for yet another score, rather than letting the clock run down. Eagles 37, Cowboys 20.

2001—Starting forward and essential defensive cog on the 76ers' 2001 NBA Finals team, George Lynch (along with Robert Traylor and Jerome Moiso) was traded by GM Billy King as part of a three-team trade for Derrick Coleman, perennial team pariah and underachiever, at the tail end of his career.

Coleman's disappointing second tour of duty with Philadelphia, coupled with Lynch's exit, historically signaled the beginning of the end of the Sixers' short-lived competitive run.

26th

1911—The Philadelphia Athletics won their second of an eventual three World Series in four years, defeating the New York Giants in Game 6, 13-2.

While it took the Phillies almost a century to win their first Series, the A's needed just under a decade (1901–1911), under the tutelage of owner/manager Connie Mack.

Aside from the 1989 earthquake-interrupted series, the 1911 championship featured the longest delay between games, as rain forced a seven-game delay between Games 3 and 4.

A consolation for those who failed to land a ticket to the Series: an impressive crowd huddled around the *New York Herald*'s "Playograph" machine, used to transmit the details of game action. (*Bain News Service*)

27th

2008—The Phillies began Game 5 of the World Series on this date, opposing the American League's Tampa Bay Rays—the final match in a culminating drive to exorcise Philadelphia's championship demons. The beginning of the end for the city's championship drought began on this day, but stormy skies and a controversial (and confusing) decision from MLB Commissioner Bud Selig would have the game's final three innings played two days later, under less hostile weather conditions.

The score would be locked at 2-2 for almost 48 hours . . .

(continued on October 29th)

COLOR COMMENTARY

Twenty-five years and counting. Finally, tonight (October 27th) was going to be our night. But was it?

I can remember the sheer anticipation that day; I was so excited to get to the ballpark that evening. I, along with every other Phillies fan, just knew that the curse would be lifted. We were going to celebrate like never before. And then something odd happened; play was suspended due to rain, making Game 5 the first game in World Series history not to be played through to completion or declared a tie.

And then it continued to rain. And rain. And rain some more. It kept raining. Game 5 started on Monday, and it didn't resume until Wednesday.

Only in Philadelphia would you have to wait through two days of rain to end a championship drought.

However, Wednesday did come, and the anticipation of victory was ramped up again. And this time, we got to see it through.

28th

1954—Major League Baseball owners rejected the sale of the Athletics to a group of Philadelphia businessmen, making clear their stance of wanting American League baseball out of the City of Brotherly Love.

Always a volatile franchise, the A's were historically big-time winners, capturing five World Series (1910–11, 1913, 1929–30), but often followed big surges with long periods of futility. With the Phillies climbing out of the cellar in 1950 to reach the World Series, and the A's mired in one of their lulls, the city of Philadelphia was no longer supporting its AL squad. And owners wanted the team out.

Eventually, the A's franchise was sold to Arnold Johnson, who moved the team to Kansas City by the start of the 1955 season.

2015—The centerpiece of the 76ers' multi-year rebuilding plan, big man Jahlil Okafor made a big splash in his NBA debut, becoming the first Sixers rookie with at least 26 points and 7 rebounds in his first game.

Okafor starred at Duke, winning a national championship during a freshman season spent mostly at the very top of most draft boards.

The young center went to the Sixers with the third pick, but Okafor looks like the prize of the draft. He will be looking to lead the Sixers' young tank-built core to new heights.

(User "TonyTheTiger," courtesy of Wikimedia Commons)

29th

2008 *(continued from October 27th)*—Christmas came early for Philly sports fans. Game 5 of the World Series concluded with a 4-3 Phillies victory, after a near-48-hour rain delay, providing a build-up and conclusion that reads like a Hollywood screenplay.

Striking out the final batter of the 2008 season, to record his 48th save on the year in as many opportunities, Brad Lidge closed out more than just a single game or season. By extorting the game's final swing-and-a-miss with the best slider in baseball, Lidge put the final touch on a moment 25 years in the making.

30th

1980—Joining Kareem Abdul-Jabbar, Elgin Baylor, Bob Cousy, John Havlicek, George Mikan, Bob Pettit, Oscar Robertson, Bill Russell, and Jerry West, Sixers greats Wilt Chamberlain and Julius Erving were elected to the NBA's All-Time team, announced to commemorate the league's 35th anniversary.

In addition, Russell was voted the best player, Red Auerbach the best coach, and the 1966–67 Sixers the best team in NBA history.

31st

2008—After a 25-year hiatus, Philadelphia played host to a championship parade. The nearly four-mile celebration started at City Hall and culminated at Citizens Bank Park, with an estimated attendance tallied at more than one million people.

And while celebrating the Phillies' remarkable season and raising the 2008 championship banner were surely unparalleled treats this Halloween day, Chase Utley had one particular trick up his sleeve for unprepared TV and radio outlets.

Scanning the crowd with the microphone in hand, Utley roared, "World f***ing champions!" to a raucous, mostly approving ovation.

Love it or hate it, Utley had stamped a fitting exclamation point on one heck of a season.

2009—With a win at Navy (27-24), the Temple University Owls football program had guaranteed its first .500-or-better season in almost 20 years.

In his fourth year at Temple, head coach Al Golden somehow turned the downtrodden program into a contender. The Owls, five years removed from being booted from the Big East Conference, and just four years from its 0-for-'05 winless campaign, finished 9-4 with an invitation to the Eaglebank Bowl (see December 29th).

For frame of reference: after going 7-4 in 1990, the Owls collected just *eight wins total* from 1991–96.

NOVEMBER

1st

2009—New York's finest took their show on the road, with the Giants taking on the Eagles in a Week 8 game at Lincoln Financial Field, followed by a Yankees-Phillies World Series Game 4 at Citizens Bank Park to cap the unique city doubleheader.

The Eagles won their end in a no-doubter, taking out the G-Men, 40-17.

The Phils, however, went down in a heartbreaker, surrendering three runs to the Yankees in the ninth inning in the 7-4 loss, to dig a 3-to-1 series hole they'd never climb out of.

2nd

1990—In a 124-116 win over the Chicago Bulls to start the 1990–91 season, Manute Bol played his first game in Philadelphia—standing at 7'7", he was the tallest player in team and league (currently tied with Gheorghe Muresan) history.

The Sudanese-born Bol, a second-round draft pick of the Washington Bullets in 1985, was a predominantly one-dimensional player in his ten-year NBA career. His immense size made for equally monolithic block totals, setting an NBA rookie record for blocks (397) in the '85–'86 season.

1998—Losing 34-0 to the Cowboys, the Eagles became the first team in NFL history to be shut out at home twice in one season by 30 points or more (the other was a 38-0 loss to the Seattle Seahawks). The epic blankings accounted for two of a franchise-record 13 losses for the Birds in 1998.

3rd

2005—During an interview with ESPN, Eagles wide receiver Terrell Owens, already steamed about his contract situation, lambasted the Eagles front office for not recognizing (or adequately celebrating) his 100th touchdown catch in a game two weeks earlier against the San Diego Chargers.

"That right there just shows you the type of class and integrity that they claim not to be," said a frustrated Owens. "They claim to be first class and the best organization. It's an embarrassment."

Later in the day, Owens was involved in a physical altercation with then–team ambassador, Hugh Douglas, which reportedly spilled out into a team-wide dispute.

While what exactly happened in the locker room between Owens and Douglas is a bit hazy, the facts remain: Owens, for a multitude of reasons, talked himself out of town.

Owens was suspended (see November 5th) for his actions and never played another game for Philadelphia.

His final game stats (10-30-2005, vs. Denver):

Three catches, 154 yards, one touchdown.

2013—Seemingly from nowhere, backup Eagles quarterback Nick Foles threw for seven touchdowns in a 49-20 victory over the Oakland Raiders.

Subbing for an injured Michael Vick, Foles compiled a perfect QB rating of 158.3, completing 78.6% of his passes for 406 yards and zero interceptions—but the key stat was the seven TDs.

Foles is one of just eight quarterbacks to accomplish the feat, along with Peyton Manning (earlier in the 2013 season), Y. A. Tittle, Joe Kapp, Sid Luckman, George Blanda, the Eagles' Adrian Burk (see October 17th), and Drew Brees.

Foles' historic day did more than just aid his chances of future starts in Eagles green. It was a sudden, portentous glimpse of potential stardom.

Foles' 119.2 QB rating in 2013 led all NFL quarterbacks. (*Philadelphia Eagles*)

4th

1960—Wilt Chamberlain took a lot of shots and broke a lot of records during his time in Philadelphia. They can't all be flattering . . .

The Big Dipper, with the Warriors, set the NBA record for most free throws attempted without registering a single point. Chamberlain's ten misses weren't crucial though, as he still put up 44 points, and the Warriors defeated the Detroit Pistons 136-121.

2009—Striking out for the 13th time, Ryan Howard broke Willie Wilson's record for most strikeouts in a single World Series.

With NLCS MVP Howard suddenly going cold and '08 World Series MVP Cole Hamels failing to rise to the occasion, the Yankees rode the hot bat of Hideki Matsui (.615 series batting average; 2.027 OPS; MVP honors) to a 7-3 victory in the deciding Game 6.

5th

2005—The Philadelphia Eagles suspended star wide receiver Terrell Owens four games without pay (the maximum under

NFL rules) for conduct detrimental to the team. The swift and severe penalty came down two days after Owens took part in an interview with ESPN, intimating the Eagles would be unbeaten on the season if Brett Favre, not Donovan McNabb, were behind center. The team deactivated T.O. after his suspension, making him unavailable to other teams.

6th

1966—Tim Brown and Aaron Martin, both return-men, scored every Eagles touchdown in a 24-23 win over the rival Dallas Cowboys.

The special teams-dominant performance for Philly included scores on two kick returns (93 and 90 yards) by Brown, and a punt return (67 yards) by Martin.

7th

1933—Philadelphia voters turned out to defeat the city's "Blue Laws," which banned professional sports in the city from being played on Sunday.

Though Philadelphia A's owner Connie Mack headed the effort, there was a lot more than a few extra Shibe Park concession dollars at stake. The Sunday law was the only thing standing in the way of the NFL's plans to place a professional football team in Philadelphia.

Their first Sunday game was the following Sunday, November 12th, against the Chicago Bears. The result? A 3-3 tie which, in addition to being the Eagles first Sunday game, was also the team's first tie.

A tie? Yes, McNabb, they have been in the rulebook for quite a while (see November 16th).

A *Puck Magazine* illustration by S. D. Ehrhart mocking the Blue Laws' contempt for Sunday sports (*Library of Congress*)

8th

1978—The Sixers beat the New Jersey Nets, 123-117, in a game that would successfully be protested by the Nets.

Because of too many assessed technical fouls, the game would be re-played with 5:50 remaining in the third quarter, over four months later (see March 23rd).

9th

1984—Forget the HBO documentary, *Magic & Bird: A Courtship of Rivals*. When you've got two of the game's top marketable stars *literally* going at each other's throats . . . that's a rivalry.

The Sixers' Julius Erving and Boston Celtics' Larry Bird came to blows in the fourth quarter of a regular season matchup on this date, in the midst of a 42-point performance by Bird, en route to a 130-119 Celts victory.

COLOR COMMENTARY

The bad blood was nothing new. Wilt Chamberlain and Bill Russell started the rivalry decades before, and rarely was there ever an important Sixers-Celtics series pre-1990 that didn't make its rounds on ESPN Classic. But Wilt and Russell never attempted dual choke-slams. That's entertainment.

2013—With both a Phillies hat and Blue Jays hat at his side, one-time Phils Ace Roy Halladay announced his retirement from Major League Baseball.

He signed a one-day contract on this date with Toronto, but announced during his press conference farewell that he wished it could have been with both teams.

In 11 seasons with the Blue Jays, Doc earned six All-Star selections, and one Cy Young Award as the American League's best pitcher.

But in just four seasons in Philadelphia, Halladay added two All-Star nods, a National League Cy Young, and two of the most dominating pitching performances in team history—his perfect game (see May 29th), and postseason no-hitter (see October 6th), both in 2010.

10th

1985—Flyers' goalie Pelle Lindbergh was killed on this date, in an automobile accident. The Vezina Trophy winner, coming off his best season as a pro, was post-humously voted in as a starter on the '86 NHL All-Star team. No Flyer has worn Lindbergh's number 31 since.

(*Philadelphia Flyers*)

COLOR COMMENTARY

Losing outcomes aside, this was the saddest I ever was as it relates to Philadelphia sports. The morning I learned of Pelle's death was only the second time in my life I had to deal with loss. The first was my grandfather; the next was Pelle. To me, they both were family.

Growing up a Flyers fan, you always knew they would contend for the Cup. You always knew they would be, most of the time, the city's best hope for glory. And the 1985–86 team had it all. Pelle was the final piece. A protégé of Bernie Parent, he had a dazzling career ahead. And then, on a cold November morning, it was gone.

I cried most of that day. I still have some remnants of the crash I keep in a scrapbook. Some 28 years later, I look back on that day, and I feel guilty for thinking his death cost

the Flyers a Cup, but now I realize that a great young life
was snuffed out because of a very poor decision.

His #31 has never been re-issued by the Flyers. It's
not retired and it doesn't hang from the rafters, but every
Flyers fan old enough to remember that faithful day
knows how very sad of a day it was.

1985—A 99-yard pass from Ron Jaworski to Mike Quick
scored the winning touchdown in a 23-17 Week 10 Eagles
overtime victory over the Atlanta Falcons.

Naturally, the pass was the longest in Eagles history and
tied an NFL record.

11th

1930—On this date, a Philadelphia team played its first game
in the National Hockey League. No, not the Flyers, but the
Quakers, a one-year castoff franchise from a bankrupt Pittsburgh squad.

The Pittsburgh Pirates franchise, the third American NHL
team, was hit hard by the Great Depression in '29, and found itself
in debt, and in sore need for serious stadium renovations. The solu-
tion? A short-term move out east to Philadelphia to capitalize on
the market until a new arena in Pittsburgh could be developed.

And while Philadelphia's long, storied competitive athletics history has seen its share of bottom-dwellers, the Quakers
were perhaps the only moribund franchise inept enough to
destroy a promising professional franchise—in a single season.

On this day in 1930, the Quakers lost 0-3 to the New
York Rangers, en route to a 4-36-4 record—a league-low

.136 winning percentage that would stand for 45 years. In response, the NHL effectively discontinued the franchise with a series of suspensions, and the Pittsburgh arena never materialized.

Not until the '67 NHL expansion would franchises return to Philadelphia and Pittsburgh.

12th

1979—In a Monday night 31-21 win over the Dallas Cowboys, barefoot kicker Tony Franklin nailed a 59-yard field goal at the end of the second half. The booming kick was the fourth-longest in league history at the time and remains an Eagles record.

1990—*The Body Bag Game.*

Making good on his promise that Washington Redskins players would "have to be carted off in body bags," head coach Buddy Ryan led his Philadelphia Eagles to a 28-14 win

COLOR COMMENTARY

It was the perfect fall evening, and it was Monday Night Football at The Vet in Philadelphia against a division rival. Talk about a perfect storm.

The Eagles came into the game trailing the Skins in the standings by a game and had already lost to Washington earlier in the season. This was a huge mid-season game, and everyone in attendance knew the Eagles were ready.

They scored two defensive touchdowns and were knocking out Washington players all over the place. It was so bad for the Skins that rookie Brian Mitchell finished the game at quarterback because the Birds already had knocked out starter Jeff Rutledge and backup Stan Humphries.

The Eagles went on to a 10-6 record for the season, and met Washington again at The Vet in the playoffs. Washington got the last laugh, winning 20-6, ending Coach Buddy Ryan's five-year run at the helm. Buddy never won a playoff game here, but this "body bag" game is one of the many reasons he will forever be loved in Philadelphia.

at the Vet on *Monday Night Football*—knocking out two quarterbacks (of eight Redskins players who were knocked out) from the game in the process. Skins kick-returner Brian Mitchell finished the game behind center.

13th

1979—76ers center Darryl Dawkins broke his first backboard as a professional player in a game that took place in Kansas City's Municipal Auditorium. A Dawkins trademark, it was the first of several for the ever-entertaining "Chocolate Thunder" that would later lead the league to install shatter-proof backboards with breakaway rims. With shards of glass nicking opposing players' legs and infiltrating the legendary afro of Julius Erving, Dawkins remarked later, "It wasn't really a safe thing to do, but it was a Darryl Dawkins thing to do."

1994—In Jeffrey Lurie's first season as owner of the Eagles, the team began perhaps its most disappointing collapse to date. Losing to the Cleveland Browns 7-26 on this date in 1994, the Birds dropped their next six games, after starting the season 7-2. The futile stretch cost head coach Rich Kotite his job—a silver lining?

1999—With a 3-2 win over the San Jose Sharks, Flyers head coach Roger Nielsen earned his 424th win (ninth in NHL history at the time) moving him past Jack Adams, the namesake for the Jack Adams Award, given to the league's top coach.

14th

1999—Taking the reins from Doug Pederson, Donovan McNabb made his first start at quarterback for the Eagles, in a Week 10 victory (35-28) over the Washington Redksins. He got the win, completing just 8-of-21 passes for 60 yards and zero touchdowns.

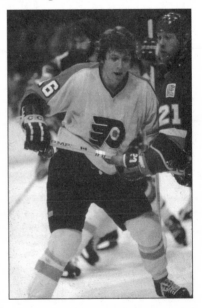

15th

1984—In his final season for the Orange & Black, Bobby Clarke, the franchise's leading scorer, was honored at the Spectrum before a 6-1 victory over the Hartford

Clarke retired his skates and took over as GM of the Flyers in 1984. (*Philadelphia Flyers*)

Whalers. The retirement of his no. 16 jersey and the unveiling of the Bobby Clarke Trophy, awarded annually to the team MVP, highlighted the Flyers' Bobby Clarke Night.

16th

1925—The Philadelphia Bobbies baseball team, the first women's team to complete a barnstorming tour of Japan (Babe Ruth's '34 tour being the most famous of any sort), played its final game, an exhibition in Kobe, on this date.

The two-and-a-half month journey for the young ladies, aged 13 to 25, was, if nothing else, an adventure. They mingled, partied, perused the culture, and, of course, played baseball. Unfortunately, the promoters reneged on their promised payments (rumored to be around $300 each), and the impact the girls had on showcasing America's pastime was relatively nil.

2008—The Eagles and Bengals kissed their sisters on this date, playing to a 13-13 tie in Week 11 of the 2008 season. A rare result, for sure, but Donovan McNabb's postgame comments made this one truly unique.

McNabb, in his ninth season as the Eagles' primary field general, was unaware that NFL games could end in ties.

"I've never been part of a tie," said a dejected McNabb. "I never even knew that was in the rulebook."

Wow.

17th

1985—In a 5-4 overtime victory over the Islanders at the Spectrum, the Flyers had won their 13th game in a row, still a team record. It is the fourth-longest streak in league history (17 games; Pittsburgh Penguins, 1993).

18th

1997—Whether you loved him or hated him during his time in Philadelphia, Bobby Abreu was a *steal*, acquired on this date via trade.

GM Ed Wade dealt light-hitting shortstop Kevin Stocker to the Tampa Bay Devil Rays for Abreu, and it didn't take long to tag the deal's winner and loser. Stocker hit .208 his first season in Tampa, while Abreu batted .312, with a .409 on-base percentage (eighth in the National league) in Phillies pinstripes.

In 2003, Abreu was voted by fans to the All-Vet Stadium Team, and played his final season in 2012.

Stocker was out of baseball by 2001 and reportedly now owns an Emerald City Smoothie franchise near Spokane, Washington.

19th

2006—Early on in this midseason 31-13 loss against the Tennessee Titans, Eagles quarterback Donovan McNabb went down with a torn ACL—a season (or two) killer. And although backup Jeff Garcia stepped up, leading the Birds into the playoffs, the long-term ramifications for McNabb were unsympathetic. Firmly stamped with the "injury-prone" tag, whispers of his demise in Philadelphia began—and continued as the team selected quarterback Kevin Kolb early in the second round of the 2007 Draft.

20th

1960—In the history of Philadelphia Eagles football, Chuck Bednarik is typically credited among the team's most devastating tacklers. Just ask New York Giants

An iconic photo, depicting Concrete Charlie celebrating over Gifford's seemingly lifeless body. (*Philadelphia Eagles*)

Hall of Fame fullback Frank Gifford.

On this date in '60, Bednarik leveled Gifford with a mammoth tackle that nearly ended the 1956 NFL MVP's career. Gifford sat out the remainder of the 1960 season and the entirety of 1961 with severe head injuries resulting from the collision. Returning in 1962 as a wide receiver, Gifford's bruising days in the trenches were over.

21st

1976—Nominated for 10 Academy Awards, including a Best Picture win, *Rocky* opened to audiences on this date in '76.

Rocky, ranked as the top sports film of all time in Ray Diddinger and Glen Macnow's *Ultimate Book*

Originally created for the film, *Rocky III,* the iconic Rocky Balboa statue rests at the Philadelphia Museum of Art. (*Michael Kirk*)

of Sports Movies, spawned five sequels, manufacturing one of Philadelphia's greatest sports heroes—Rocky Balboa.

22nd

Neale, Cincinnati Reds, 1917
(Bain News Service)

1920—In a swap of pitchers, the Phillies sent lefty Eppa Rixey to the Cincinnati Reds for righty Jimmy Ring. As part of the deal, the Phils also got an outfielder who would eventually become a Hall of Famer—*Pro Football* Hall of Famer, Greasy Neale.

Alfred Earle "Greasy" Neale, College and Pro Football Hall of Fame coach, and the only Eagles skipper to win two championships, played sparsely for the Phillies at the tail end of a respectable eight-year Major League career.

23rd

1954—In an announcement made at Penn's Houston Hall, university president Dr. Gaylord Harnwell introduced the formation of the Big 5.

Robert S. Lyons said it best in his book, *Palestra Pandemonium: A History of the Big 5—*

For more than three decades, Philadelphia Big 5—LaSalle, Pennsylvania, St. Joseph's, Temple and Villanova—waged college basketball's biggest, most envied, unique, and frenetic, intracity rivalry. No other city in the nation ever had as many major universities competing so feverishly for such a coveted title as did the City of Brotherly Love.

24th

1892—Central High and Northeast High School in Philadelphia started a local tradition that is as synonymous with Thanksgiving as turkey and bickering in-laws. To be fair, it may not have been the first Thanksgiving Day game on American soil (the first possibly taking place between Wellesley and Needham High schools in Massachusetts?), but the tradition is certainly one of the oldest.

1960—On this date, Wilt Chamberlain of the Philadelphia Warriors played his self-proclaimed *greatest game*. And it wasn't the 100-pointer or the 20-20-20 game.

Most surprising of all is that it came in a *loss,* to the Boston Celtics, 132-129.

The Big Dipper grabbed an NBA-record 55 rebounds in a losing effort on this date, while matched up against the league's premier team (Boston) and best all-time big man not named Wilt Chamberlain (Bill Russell). And with that, it's no wonder Chamberlain considered it his best individual performance.

The mutual respect between the two—Chamberlain and Russell—was an inevitable result of their situation. They played the same position, for rival teams, contributing at such tremendously higher levels on both offense and defense than the game had ever previously seen.

Chamberlain may have lost that night, but his rival brought out the best in him.

"We competed against each other probably more intensely than we did against anybody else because if you didn't take it to the level that you had to take it, you would be embarrassed," Russell said. "And none of us wanted that. So I think we probably played harder against each other than we did against anybody else."

25th

2007—Out of nowhere, backup quarterback A. J. Feeley, subbing for the injured Donovan McNabb, nearly led the Eagles to an upset victory over the 10-0 New England Patriots, as a 23 ½ point underdog.

Feeley passed for 345 yards and three touchdowns, leading late against the Patriots, who would ultimately end up as the only team in NFL history to finish with a perfect 16-0 regular season.

Feeley also threw three interceptions in the game, ironically landing him with an almost identical stat line to Donovan McNabb in the team's three-point loss to New England in Super Bowl XXXIX (357 yds/3 TD/3 INT).

"Three points. The Patriots and three points," bemoaned Eagles coach Andy Reid after the 31-28 loss, "They're killing me."

26th

1964—Who holds the single-game scoring record *against* the 76ers? The same guy who holds seemingly every scoring record *for* the team—Wilton Norman Chamberlain.

Before his days in Sixers duds, Wilt Chamberlain went off for 63 points in the San Francisco Warriors' 128-117 *loss* to the 76ers.

27th

1949—You'll see a couple per season these days, but back in 1949, the Eagles' Steve Van Buren was the first running back in 16 years, and second player overall (Cliff Battles, 215 yards; 1933), to rush for over 200 yards in a single game, collecting 205 yards in a 34-17 victory over the Pittsburgh Steelers.

The record had staying power. In 2013, Van Buren's single game tally was finally bested, with a 217-yard effort by LeSean McCoy (see December 8th).

28th

1997—In a 4-1 victory over the New York Islanders in the annual Black Friday Matinee game, the Flyers debuted their first alternate jersey in team history. Following some solid showings in the jersey, the Flyers upgraded the black-dominant alternates to the primary road jersey during the 2001–'02/2002–'03 seasons.

29th

1998—Flyers great John LeClair had, arguably, his best individual game for the Orange & Black, scoring four goals in a 6-2 win over the Vancouver Canucks. In addition, LeClair tied a franchise record in the contest, scoring three goals in a single (third) period.

30th

1997—Bobby Hoying, upstart Eagles quarterback, threw four touchdown passes in a thrilling 44-42 Week 14 win over the Cincinnati Bengals. Those four TDs carried heavy expectations for the suddenly touted "savior" going into the 1998 season—his last as a starting quarterback in the NFL.

Forget four in a single game; in his seven starts in 1998, Hoying would fail to throw a single touchdown pass.

1st

1974—The Flyers defeated the Kansas City Scouts, 10-0, in a game in which eight different players scored for Philadelphia. Bobby Clarke tied the team record at the time for assists in a single game (four) and the team as a whole tied the record (since broken in an 11-0 victory over the Penguins in '77) for the largest shutout victory in franchise history.

The win was the second in a 12-game unbeaten streak— one of many, as the Flyers finished the regular season at 51-18-11 and went on to capture their second straight Stanley Cup.

2nd

1990—One of the most dazzling plays in Philadelphia sports history occurred on this date, as Eagles QB Randall Cunningham eluded a pass rush in his own end zone and connected for a 95-yard touchdown pass to Fred Barnett.

Cunningham was at his best in 1990, his MVP year (Pro Football Writers Association), and this was the signature play of his season and career. Dropping back into a rapidly collapsing pocket, Cunningham evaded a defender in front, then, somehow, ducked to avoid a sack from behind—with his back turned to Bruce Smith, the would-be tackler. He then rolled out to a clearance and, while still in the end zone, hurled a bomb (with sixty yards of hang time) to Barnett, who ran the rest of the way for the 95-yard score.

The Birds would lose the game to the Buffalo Bills, 30-23, but Cunningham's *Matrix*-like maneuver has since made the score irrelevent.

3rd

1950—The Cleveland Browns beat the Eagles, 13-7, in the last game, likely ever, in which a team (the Browns) did not attempt a single pass.

Oddly, the Browns rushed for just under two yards per carry, accumulating only 69 yards of total offense, yet still got the win. A 30-yard interception return by Cleveland defensive back Warren Lahr scored Cleveland's only touchdown.

4th

1964—Major League Baseball approved the first Free Agent Amateur Draft in league history.

Performed in the summer of '65, teams drafted in the reverse order of where they finished during the regular season, with 824 total players selected. The Phillies' first selection with the 18th overall pick was right-hander Mike Adamson, who never pitched in Philadephia.

Who did the Phillies pass on? Nolan Ryan, Tom Seaver, Johnny Bench, Graig Nettles, Hal McRae, and Darrell Evans were all selected in later rounds.

5th

1998—During play of the 99th Army-Navy Game at Veterans Stadium, a railing collapsed, injuring eight cadets who were celebrating against the shoddy structure after Army had taken the lead late, 31-30. It was an important precursor to the planning and construction of the Eagles' Lincoln Financial Field, and the Phils' Citizens Bank Park.

2004—On this date, Donovan McNabb had, arguably, his greatest game as quarterback for the Eagles. Breaking Joe Montana's streak of consecutive complete passes (10 in this game, coupled with 14 to end the previous contest), McNabb threw for five

McNabb, amidst a smattering of boos, taking the stage at the 1999 NFL Draft. (*Philadelphia Eagles*)

touchdowns and a team-record 464 yards in the Birds' 47-17 rout of the Green Bay Packers.

The one-year anniversary would go a little different . . .

2005—Already 5-6 on the season, with Donovan McNabb on Injured Reserve, the Eagles had little but pride on the line in their matchup with the eventual NFC champion Seattle Seahawks on *Monday Night Football*. The result was a 42-0 stomping by Seattle, capping the disappointment on a lost Eagles season.

The third-worst defeat in team history was on display for the world to see. At the time, it was tied for the most lopsided contest in *Monday Night Football* history.

6th

2006—Starving for depth in the starting rotation, Phillies brass pulled the trigger on a move to bring in Freddy Garcia, a 17-game winner for the Chicago White Sox the season prior. Giving up top prospect starter Gavin Floyd, along with current Washington Nationals ace Gio Gonzalez as a throw-in, the Phils got just one win out of their $10 million investment in the DL-bound Garcia. Meanwhile, Floyd would win 17 games for Chicago in 2008, while Gonzalez finished third in the NL Cy Young voting in 2012.

7th

1994—Jeff Malone scored a game-high 34 points during a 111-102 win over the Miami Heat as the 76ers joined the LA Lakers and Boston Celtics in rare company, becoming the third NBA franchise to reach the 2,000 victory mark.

While the 1994–95 team hit the number, the Sixers owe the honor to its championship teams of seasons past. After all, the team's 64 combined wins in three seasons from 1994–95 to 1996–97 was *four games less* than the team's 68 wins in 1966–67 alone.

8th

1945—Widely considered the top high school playoff football game in city history, and voted the greatest high school sporting event ever played in Philadelphia (according to a *Daily News* panel in 1986), Southern defeated West Catholic, 18-13, for the city title in 1945.

Southern scored three touchdowns in the final 7:40 (do the math—that's *zero* successful extra point attempts), with the winning score coming by way of an 11-yard touchdown pass, kicker-to-holder, on a fake field goal attempt.

In an interview with Ted Silary 50 years later, kicker Anthony Coletta broke down the final play:

Coach (Joe) Pitt decided to run a fake field goal. He told the ends to run a crisscross and told me, "See if you can spot somebody." I was being rushed, of course, real hard, and it got

to be one of those schoolyard, two-hand-touch plays where
you just run around goofy, zigzagging.

I spotted Al (Tulinsky) at the 5. Wide open! He caught it
and ran in. No problem.

An estimated 54,000 fans witnessed the classic at Franklin Field, at a time when high school football in Philadelphia was a big draw.

1987—Rookie Ron Hextall, Vezina Trophy winner as the league's top goaltender in 1986–87, shot and scored a goal—the first ever for a goalie in league history.

Known for his stick handling and sharp passing ability, Hextall would do it again in 1989, owning two of just seven goals ever put in the net by a goaltender.

The Flyers won the game, 5-2, over the Boston Bruins.

(Philadelphia Flyers)

COLOR COMMENTARY

I was 16 at the time, and a Flyers nut. I remember back in '87, we only had one television in the house that had cable, and the team's home games were covered by PRISM. My father was not a sports fan, and I remember absolutely begging him to watch the Flyers that evening. He finally relented, and I got to view history.

> For the prior three months, Hextall had been threatening to accomplish this feat that hadn't been done before in the history of the NHL. Gene Hart, the Flyers announcer, always said that the situation had to be perfect, that the team needed to be up by two, and Hextall needed a clear chute. He got them both and turned a regular season victory over the Bruins into a memory of a lifetime for many.

2013—Unexpectedly relentless snowfall pounded Lincoln Financial Field, setting the scene for an exciting and unforgettable 34-20 Eagles victory over the Detroit Lions in Week 14 of the NFL season.

Near white-out conditions played a key role in stalling the Eagles' high-powered offense early, as they managed negative two yards of total offense through the first quarter of play.

But key adjustments ignited the Eagles' offensive attack, with running back Lesean "Shady" McCoy leading a historical second-half charge that accounted for all 34 Birds points.

Dashing through the snow, McCoy effortlessly cut and slashed through Detroit's defense like his cleats were clad with snow chains. In all, Shady amassed a team-record 217 rushing yards, eclipsing Steve Van Buren's total of 205 set 64 years prior.

The win was the fifth in a row for Philadelphia and rookie coach, Chip Kelly. The team's 8-5 record to that point doubled their win total of the previous year.

(Philadelphia Eagles/Drew Hallowell)

9th

1982—The Phillies liked Von Hayes' five-tool potential so much that they traded five players (Julio Franco, George Vukovich, Manny Trillo, Jay Baller, and Jerry Willard) to acquire the lanky outfielder, nicknamed "5-for-1" (or "541") by teammate Pete Rose. The moniker, in jest, stuck with Hayes, who, perhaps unfairly, was suddenly burdened with the responsibility to over-perform.

In reality, Hayes was a serviceable outfielder in Philadelphia—reliable, if not remarkable. If Julio Franco hadn't been part of the deal—a 23-year Major League veteran with a .298 career batting average—Philadelphia fans may have let Hayes off the hook.

10th

1950—Greasy Neale coached his final game for the Philadelphia Eagles, a 7-9 loss to the New York Giants. A College and Pro Football Hall of Fame coach, Neale compiled a career 63-43-5 record with the Birds, winning three straight Eastern Division crowns and two championships (1948, '49).

The loss was the fourth straight for the Eagles (6-6), in a season in which they also had a string of five straight *victories*.

1961—Eagles Hall of Fame wide receiver Tommy McDonald set a team record for receiving yards with 237, in a Week 13 loss to the New York Giants, 28-24. Fellow Hall of Famer Sonny Jurgensen (though he spent most of his career with the Washington Redskins), enjoying his first Pro Bowl season, had 367 yards passing in the losing effort, en route to a league-leading 3,723 on the year.

11th

1969—Kate Smith made her debut for the Flyers—well, her recording of "God Bless America" did anyway.

Smith, a popular recording artist of the '30s and '40s, was the original voice of the Irving Berlin classic. Trying to mix things up, the Flyers substituted her rendition in place of "The Star-Spangled Banner," a move that wasn't an immediate hit with hockey fans. And while it may have offended some to omit the country's national anthem, Smith's "God Bless America" came with an interesting peace offering: Flyers wins.

When the song played, the Flyers couldn't lose. That's how the team felt, anyway. As the wins mounted (65-13-2 at the Spectrum when the song played), the good-luck charm had validation. Superstitious players on both sides of the ice bought into the hype, creating a very real psychological edge for Philadelphia.

California Seals coach Vic Stasiuk, in a playoff push with the Flyers in 1972, said about their late-season matchup with Philadelphia, "Now if they don't use Kate Smith, we'll be alright." Smith ran her record to 21-2-1 that night, as the Flyers defeated the Seals, 3-0.

During the first six years of this tradition, from 1969 to 1975, the Flyers were a brilliant 43-3-1.

Smith, 1925 (*Library of Congress*)

12th

2005—Chris Webber's time in Philadelphia was remembered most for his debilitating contract and damaged knees. It's hard to remember that he actually had a few sparks of respectability with the 76ers.

In a 90-89 OT win over the Minnesota Timberwolves, C-Webb scored a game-high 27 points with 21 rebounds.

"I'm not by any means dead yet," insisted Webber after the game. "I want the opportunity to play that way every night."

After two more lackluster seasons, Webber was out of the league.

13th

1994—The 76ers' Willie Burton became the most unlikely 50-point scorer in NBA history, dropping 53 in total on the Heat in a 105-90 Philly win. He shot 12-19 from the field and 24-28 from the free throw line.

According to BasketballProspectus.com, Burton's 3,243 career points total ranks as the lowest for a non-active 50-point scorer. Who's scored the most NBA points without ever registering a 50-pointer?

Hall of Famers John Havlicek (26,395), Charles Barkley (23,757), and Robert Parish (23,334), just to name a few.

14th

1994—The Phillies signed Gregg Jefferies, who hit .342 and .325, respectively, his previous two seasons in St. Louis, to the largest contract in franchise history at the time—four years, $20 million.

The Jefferies signing is largely viewed as a bust, and his lack of power at a corner outfield position at the dawn of the "steroid era" would certainly support that viewpoint. But he did hit .292 or higher three times in four years with the squad—something the likes of Mike Schmidt, Ryan Howard, and Jimmy Rollins never accomplished even once.

15th

1968—One might think it's an annual holiday ritual in Philadelphia, the way the national media constantly brings it up, but the day Eagles fans pelted Santa with snowballs actually occurred way back on this date, at halftime of an eventual 24-17 loss to the Minnesota Vikings.

Because of a snowstorm, the originally contracted Santa couldn't make it to the game, and the float he was to ride onto the field was too heavy to slosh through the muddied Franklin Field grass. What *did* make it onto the field that day was an unsuspecting understudy, ill-prepared to look and play the part of everyone's favorite jolly ole' Saint.

Only brief grainy personal video footage survives today, but according to reports, 20-year-old Eagles fan Frank Olivo, dressed as Santa of his own accord, marched the length of the field under the Birds' request, tattered suit and all.

There was no float. Aside from "Here Comes Santa Claus" blasting through the stadium, there were no yuletide seasonal aids.

Simply, the 5'6" 170-lb Olivo was fed to the firing squad.

COLOR COMMENTARY

Over the years, this event has often been referenced when out of town reporters/commentators seek to quantify the integrity of the Eagles' faithful fan base. But it's usually lazy and under-informed reporting.

"Remember, they booed Santa Clause" is how it's often tee'd up. Which is ironic, because who actually remembers? It was almost 50 years ago, and the video evidence is scarce. What people remember are the irresponsible retellings that skew facts into fiction at the expense of the Philadelphia fan.

1973—Tennessee beat Temple, 11-6—that's not a typo—in the lowest-scoring game in NCAA Men's Basketball history.

In a pre–shot clock standoff (it wouldn't be introduced in College Basketball until after Villanova's Tournament victory in '85), Temple held the ball for 32 of the 40 minutes, waiting for the Tennessee zone to dissolve—which it never did.

"Austin Clark kind of ventured out [of the zone] a few times," said Vols point guard Rodney Woods of his teammate, "and I remember them [Head Coach Ray Mears, and assistants] threatening to kill him if he didn't get back and keep things tight."

2010—*Merry Cliffmas!* Righting what seemed to be a flagrant wrong, the Phillies signed Cliff Lee on this date to a $120 million contract, one season after a controversial blindside trade by Philadelphia landed Lee in Seattle.

Lee was originally traded to make room in the budget for signing free agent Roy Halladay (see December 16th).

16th

1979—After compiling 60 rushing yards in a 26-20 defeat of the Houston Oilers in the final game of the regular season, Wilbert Montgomery established a single-season team record (1,512 yards) that would stand for 34 years.

The Eagles have had a great string of running backs during the '90s and '00s—think Ricky Watters, Duce Staley, Brian Westbrook, and LeSean McCoy. It might be easy to forget that by the conclusion of the 1981 season, Montgomery had owned the top three rushing yardage seasons in team history.

Then, in 2013, McCoy supplanted Montgomery atop the leader board with a brilliant 1,607-yard performance. Another season like that, and Shady will tackle Montgomery's 6,538-yard Eagles career record as well.

1995—After serving three years in prison on a rape charge, Mike Tyson was back in the ring, roughing up Buster Mathis, Jr. at the Spectrum in Philadelphia in his final tune-up.

Ultimately, Tyson had his sights set on Frank Bruno and his WBC belt (which he'd win), but Mathis was no cupcake. Surviving two rounds—an eternity, in Tyson's heyday—Mathis was knocked out by Iron Mike, on an uppercut, in Round 3.

The fight, which aired on FOX (do they show big fights on cable anymore?), earned a respectable rating, reportedly reeling in more than 43 million viewers, despite Tyson's 90-second knockout of Peter McNeeley four months earlier, which fell far short of its lofty billing.

2009—The Phillies landed the best pitcher in baseball in Roy Halladay—at the cost of the team's former ace, Cliff Lee.

Halladay, a Cy Young winner with the Toronto Blue Jays, cost the Phillies three of their top prospects. Lee himself cost the Phils *four* prospects at the trade deadline in '08, so rather than ride out the last year of Lee's contract on a one-season splurge, the Phils chose to deal Lee to the Seattle Mariners to restock the farm system.

In return, the Phils acquired fringe prospects Phillippe Aumont, Tyson Gillies, and J. C. Ramirez. Oops.

One year later, Lee rejoined the club, pitching behind the 2010 Cy Young winner, Halladay.

17th

1978—*Happy Birthday, Chase Utley!* One of the most popular and perhaps the finest second baseman to ever wear the red and white pinstripes for the Philadelphia Phillies was born on this day. Utley, whose first hit in the big leagues was a grand slam off of Colorado's Aaron Cook at Veterans Stadium, is admired most by the fans for his hard-nosed style of play, and infamous for his expletive "World f***ing champions" statement delivered while greeting the fans during the team's 2008 championship celebration.

18th

1949—The Eagles defeated the LA Rams, 14-0, for the NFL Championship, their second (consecutive) in team history.

Eagles running back Steve Van Buren contributed 196 rushing yards in the victory, a postseason record that stood for nearly 40 years.

The Eagles have three NFL Championships in hand (1948–49, 1960), but, of course, no Super Bowls.

19th

1948—During blizzard conditions at Shibe Park in Philadelphia, 36,309 fans braved the storm to witness the Eagles win their first NFL Championship, 7-0, over the Chicago Cardinals.

Hall of Fame running back Steve Van Buren scored the only touchdown of the game, in the fourth quarter, after a Cards fumble turned over a short field.

Legend has it, Van Buren had initially stayed home, assuming the game would not be played in such brutal conditions. When the commissioner allowed the teams to play (ironically, by request of both teams' players), Van Buren ultimately had to walk the last seven blocks to the park in knee-deep snow (uphill both ways?) to make it to the game on time.

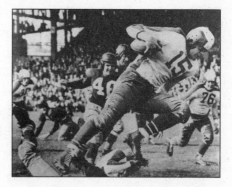

Van Buren was among the most dominant forces in football in the 1940s. *(Philadelphia Eagles)*

2004—12-1 and running away with the division, the Eagles played what turned out to be a monumental contest for both the franchise and the league. On this date in 2004, Dallas Cowboys cornerback Roy Williams "horse-collar" tackled wide receiver Terrell Owens, sidelining him for the remainder of the regular season and NFC playoffs. As serious injuries to premiere players often have a habit of doing, the league outlawed the tackle the following offseason. As of 2009, Roy Williams has been the most penalized abuser of the aptly named "Roy Williams Rule."

The Eagles won the contest, 12-7.

2006—There are very few sweet farewells when an icon departs. Such was certainly the case when Allen Iverson was traded on this day (along with Ivan McFarlin) to the Denver Nuggets for Andre Miller, Joe Smith, and two first-round draft picks (Daequan Cook and Petteri Koponen). With the decade-long face of the franchise gone—in hopes to start over and rebuild for the betterment of the team—for most, there was an uneasy feeling.

In a league where, seemingly, the only quick fixes come by way of "lottery" draft picks, trading Iverson was no guarantee for future success—it wasn't even a reasonable probability.

In fact, by landing Andre Miller in return, an All-Star-caliber point guard while in his prime, the Sixers perhaps did not get bad enough to land a high draft pick and climb out of mediocrity.

2014—The Phillies traded shortstop Jimmy Rollins to the Los Angeles Dodgers, in a deal for pitchers Zach Efflin and Tom Windle. The Phillies' career hits leader (2,306) won four Gold Gloves and an MVP award (2007) with the club, and leads nearly every offensive category for the Phillies from the shortstop position. His 2,422 hits, so far, are the 10th-most among primary shortstops in baseball history.

Said longtime teammate Chase Utley on the move:

"The Dodgers are very lucky to acquire a player like Jimmy... Jimmy makes everyone around him better. The team will miss his leadership on the field and his infectious smile, but most of all, I will miss our pre-game handshake."

(*Kevin Durso*)

20th

2004—Allen Iverson put up his second straight 50-point game on this date, in a 103-101 loss to the Utah Jazz.

After dropping 54 points on the Milwaukee Bucks, Iverson sank 18 field goals for 51 points against the Utah Jazz, and even flashed a little defensive prowess, getting seven steals in the process.

Iverson became the only 76er in franchise history to go for 50 points in two straight games, and since, no Sixer has done it even *once*.

21st

1849—The Skater's Club of the City and County of Philadelphia formed on this date, the first known club of its kind in the United States.

According to the club's website (pschs.org):

The club's objectives were "instruction and improvement" in the art of skating, cultivation of a friendly feeling in all who participated in the amusement of skating, and efficient use of proper apparatus for the rescue of persons breaking through the ice.

The club dissolved within a few years, but led the way for The Philadelphia Skating Club and Humane Society, established in 1861.

22nd

1862—On this date, Cornelius McGillicuddy, aka Connie Mack, the Philadelphia A's owner/manager, and perhaps most influential sports figure in Philadelphia, was born in East Brookfield, Massachusetts.

The Tall Tactician predated the Major Leagues, but by the time of his death in 1956, he brought American League baseball to Philadelphia, won the city's first *five* championships (before the Phillies mustered one), and pushed his weight around for 50 years in a quest to make Philadelphia the center of the professional baseball universe.

Ultimately, the city wasn't big enough for two titans, and the A's were sold to leave Philadelphia solely in the hands of the National League Phillies. But how's this for respect: even though they were crosstown rivals, the Phillies continued to play in the aptly named Connie Mack Stadium, and even erected a statue of Mack that currently sits outside their Citizens Bank Park home.

23rd

1958—Add Sparky Anderson to the list of Hall of Fame coaches who once played for the Phillies.

On this date, the Phillies traded Jim Golden, Rip Repulski, and Gene Snyder for the infielder Anderson, who would play his only Major League season in 1959, before a 26-year managerial career that included two championships with the Big Red Machine in Cincinnati and one with the Detroit Tigers.

Casey Stengal, Greasy Neale (NFL), and Tommy Lasorda also spent time in the Phillies organization before their Hall of Fame coaching careers elsewhere.

24th

1978—The Eagles were ahead 13-0 in the fourth quarter of the opening round playoff matchup with the Atlanta Falcons. What followed were two quick strikes late by Atlanta; led by quarterback Steve Bartkowski and with less than two minutes remaining, the Falcons had a 14-13 lead. But that's not the part of the collapse people remember.

Eagles quarterback Ron Jaworski led a clutch drive down to the Falcons 16-yard line with just seconds remaining. Needing just a chip shot field goal to win it, punter-turned-kicker Mike Michel shanked it. Game over. The Falcons won, 14-13.

It is still my earliest memory of Eagles football. It was Christmas Eve, Santa was coming, and I was happily watching playoff football. But, the Scrooge stepped in and cancelled any celebration.

I didn't know who Mike Michel was. I had just turned eight years old two days prior and really didn't fully understand the implications and the effect this game had on the fan base.

Years later, I realized, this one hurt badly. How could Dick Vermeil not sign a veteran kicker? How could he allow someone who has never attempted a FG in his career to do so for the first time in the playoffs?

Michel missed an extra point, a 42-yarder, and then the chip shot to win it. I would've loved hosting that postgame show!

25th

1986—The 76ers' Christmas gift to the Washington Bullets came back to haunt them.

Moses Malone, the hero of the 1983 Championship team, traded the previous June to the Bullets (see June 16th), made his return to Philadelphia on Christmas Day for the first time against his former team, scoring 28 points to go with 21 rebounds and five blocks, in a 102-97 win over Philly.

Clearly, he had a lot left in the tank.

Malone sadly passed away on September 13, 2015 at the age of 60.

26th

1960—Even the day *after* Christmas has brought some truly memorable and remarkable gifts to Philadelphia sports fans.

On this day in 1960, the Philadelphia Eagles won their last NFL Championship. It was the league's 28th title game, played six years before the sport would see its first Super Bowl. And while the accomplishment is dwarfed by the immense spectacle that has become the Super Bowl—far and away America's top sporting event—it is still a worthy championship notch on the franchise's belt.

Led by Hall of Famers Chuck Bednarik, Norm Van Brocklin, and Tommy McDonald, the Eagles defeated the Green Bay Packers, 17-13, despite being outgained in yardage, 401-296. Bednarik tackled Packers running back Jim Taylor eight yards short of the end zone to end the game. He was the sole Eagles defender between Taylor and what would have been a game-winning score for Green Bay.

It turned out to be Hall of Famer Vince Lombardi's first and only playoff loss as a coach in the NFL.

27th

1987—In a 17-7 win over the Buffalo Bills, the Eagles' greatest defensive player, Reggie White, recorded his team-record 20th and 21st sacks of the season.

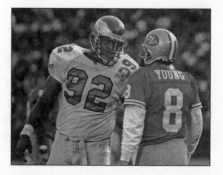

A 10-time First-Team All-Pro, White was a quarterback's worst nightmare. *(Phildelphia Eagles)*

At the time, his sack total was an NFL single-season record, and he accomplished the feat in just 12 games. Naturally, White was an obvious choice at season's end for the Defensive Player of the Year award.

2003—The Eagles secured a first-round bye in the playoffs with a 31-7 win over the Washington Redskins. The story of the game? Running back Brian Westbrook's triceps injury that would keep him out of the season's remaining games—including the 14-3 loss to the Panthers for the team's third straight NFC Championship defeat. To add insult to injury (literally), Westbrook's wound was incurred on a tackle by none other than Washington linebacker Jeremiah Trotter, a fan favorite while with Philadelphia.

28th

1947—Before the Eagles notched their first championship victory over the Chicago Cardinals in 1948 (7-0), they lost to the Cards, 28-21, in their first-ever NFL title game in '47.

Unlike the Birds' NFC Championship woes in the 2000s, the Birds of the '40s didn't repeat their initial failures. The Eagles would return to the championship game in '48 and '49, winning both of them under legendary head coach Greasy Neale.

29th

2009—In Temple's first bowl game since 1979, the UCLA Bruins handed the Owls a 30-21 defeat in the EagleBank Bowl.

The season was a success, however, for fourth-year coach Al Golden, who led the Owls to their first winning season since 1990.

Too much too soon? Golden's historic resurrection of Temple Football made bigger programs take notice. Following the 2010 season, Golden agreed to coach the prestigious, though flawed, Miami Hurricanes.

2015—Eagles owner Jeffrey Lurie shocked Birds fans, and the nation, firing third-year head coach Chip Kelly with one

COLOR COMMENTARY

In what many people described as shocking, I somewhat felt it was inevitable. There were just too many changes, and not enough wins for Kelly to survive. When Chip was first hired three seasons prior, I was ecstatic. I really believed in him and that his successes in college would translate to big things in the NFL. Sadly, however, halfway through his final season, I came to the conclusion that this experiment, or risk, was not going to work out.

Eagles Owner Jeffrey Lurie, in his explaining his decision: "I have made a decision to release Chip Kelly this evening. I spent the last three seasons evaluating the many factors involved in our performance as a team. As I watched this season unfold, I determined that it was time to make a change."

Jeffrey Lurie is not the most popular figure in Philadelphia. Some of his decisions have been severely questioned, but in this case, he made the right call. Lurie knew the damage done by Kelly's personnel moves were gaining momentum and he absolutely needed to take back control of his franchise.

game remaining in the 2015 regular season. The Eagles were 10-6 in consecutive seasons with Chip Kelly at the helm, but sputtered to 6-9 at the time of his release.

Lurie, in a press conference following the move, acknowledged Kelly had some success, but noted "the end result was mediocrity."

"This was one of the most disappointing seasons I've ever endured. Surprising, I thought we were on the verge of something special."

Lurie's sentiments couldn't have been more in sync with frustrated Eagles fans everywhere.

30th

1943—The Phillies and Pirates traded "Babes" and neither one was a "Ruth."

The Phils traded first baseman Babe Dahlgren to the Pittsburgh Pirates for catcher Babe Phelps on this date in '43. The

COLOR COMMENTARY

This is the perfect example of the Phillies' backward dealing that left them constantly fighting to stay out of last place for much of the century. They traded a 31-year-old all-star in Dahlgren not for prospects, but, literally, a retired player. Dahlgren got MVP votes for a 90-win Pirates squad in 1944. The Phillies finished dead last.

deal was the last time two *Babes* were traded for each other until Brad dumped Jen for Angelina...

But seriously . . . Dahlgren had a great season for Pittsburgh in 1944 (.289/12 HR/101), while Phelps never came off the voluntarily retired list for the Phils.

31st

1990—In a 133-118 win over Loyola Marymount, La Salle put on one of the most impressive offensive performances in city collegiate history. La Salle set team records for most combined points of two and three teammates, respectively, in the same game (91, 120, respectively).

Randy Woods (46), Doug Overton (45), and Jack Hurd (29), all hitting career highs, accounted for about 90% of La Salle's total points.

COLOR COMMENTARY

La Salle has the top two players in combined points and rebounds in men's college basketball history—Tom Gola (4,663) and Lionel Simmons (4,646).

It's surprising that such a historically high-scoring game in La Salle's history does not include Simmons. Having jumped to the NBA in 1990, Simmons finished his Explorers career with 3,217 points, good for third all-time in NCAA men's basketball history.

REFERENCES

The Eagles Encyclopedia; Ray Didinger, Robert S. Lyons

Flyershistory.net

Flyers.nhl.com

Full Spectrum; Jay Greenberg

The Great Book of Philadelphia Sports Lists; Glen Macnow, Big Daddy Graham

The Library of Congress

Philadelphiaeagles.com

Philadelphiaphillies.com

The Phillies Encyclopedia; Rich Westcott, Frank Bilovsky

Sixers.com

Sportsecyclopedia.com

Sports-reference.net

Todayinsport.com

INDEX